MARY SEACOLE

RON RAMDIN is a historian, biographer and novelist. He was honoured as a Pioneer by the Windrush Foundation in 2018. Ramdin's previous books include *The Making of the Black Working Class in Britain* (2017) and the novels *The Griot's Tale* (2009) and *Or Not to Be: The True Story of William Shakespeare* (2020). He lives in London.

MARY SEACOLE

RON RAMDIN

First published in Great Britain in 2005 by
Haus Publishing Ltd
4 Cinnamon Row
London SW11 3TW
www.hauspublishing.com

This second paperback edition published in 2020

A CIP catalogue record for this book is available from the British Library

ISBN 978-1-913368-09-8
eISBN 978-1-913368-34-0

Typeset in Garamond by MacGuru Ltd

Printed in the United Kingdom by Clays Ltd, Elcograf S.p.A.

Contents

Early Life

Mary Seacole was born in Kingston, capital of the British island of Jamaica, in 1805. She did not give us this year herself, nor the precise day or month of her birth. She was shy of divulging such details and, in response to the question in later life, she wrote that 'as a female and a widow, I may be well excused giving the precise date of this important event. But I do not mind confessing that the century and myself were both young together and [...] we have grown side by side into age and consequence.'[1]

In the early 19th century, race was a major issue in Jamaica. Early researchers have commented that in order to fully understand Mary Seacole's achievements, her work must be measured against the time in which she lived and the restrictions under which she had to operate. In 1807, two years after her birth, Britain had abolished the slave trade, but the institution of slavery persisted. When it came to civil rights in Jamaican society at this time, skin colour was all important, and throughout her childhood and for the rest of her life, Mary would have been aware of its relevance. According to Rex Nettleford, for those aspiring to become citizens, 'the most difficult obligation of all in the scheme of preparation would have been the dilution of colour. It took three generations to become a Jamaican white by law.'[2] Those wishing to gain social ascendancy were careful to choose partners 'to ensure that offsprings would enjoy in the next generation, what Free Coloured or black mothers could not in their own.'[3]

Mary Seacole was the child of that class in Jamaica known as the 'Free Coloureds' who 'helped to perpetuate the very basis on which the majority of the population [who were black] were denied that freedom.'[4] Indeed, the free people of colour of Jamaica were placed in a paradoxical situation at this time, unlike the enslaved black people who had to fight for freedom of expression and allied rights. Although the free people of colour could express themselves through the process of free exchange – for example, petitioning – they did so on limited terms. But, importantly, they were free people in a slave society, and as such the 'distinction had to be made between the slave and free men, despite the fact that one set of free men (Whites) made little or no distinction between another set of free men (Free Coloureds) and slaves.'[5] Many free people of colour were, like white people, owners of property, including enslaved people. They believed implicitly in slaveholding and were against abolition. While many petitions were governed by law, some were embodied in customs and conventions; thus, the hierarchy of colour found expression in both, 'giving legitimacy to carefully measured drops of white blood that flowed in the veins of Free Coloureds. The acquisition of privileges would *ipso facto* mean the elevation to whiteness which was in any case necessary to determine eligibility for rights and privileges – a vicious circle.'[6] Whites used the 'Free Coloured' class as a buffer between themselves and the potentially rebellious enslaved black people. Nonetheless, this gave most free people of colour a sense of purpose despite their disadvantages. It was through this system of special privileges that many free people of colour were able to gain access to some of society's channels of advancement. And by reason of growing wealth, many free people of colour could travel to England and establish connections with articulate and fairly influential persons, including politicians. The trouble was that, in their fight for freedom of expression and other civil rights, free people of colour in early 19th-century Creole Jamaica failed to commit themselves to a belief in the prudence or necessity of universal privileges. As a group, at this time of slavery, the Free Coloureds seemed to have lacked anything approaching an independent ideology for freedom. They made the unpardonable error of insisting that they were eligible for freedom because they too were of white blood. Their stand was even more outrageous because the white people in their midst did not regard them as white and did all they could to ensure that any elevation to that much-coveted ethnic status would take no fewer than three generations. 'The Creolization process was itself further distorted by the integration into the very process of the dependency syndrome, the imitative ideal,' as Nettleford put it, 'and the notion that what was white was right and what came from black thought much less so.'[7] Thus free people of colour committed an error of judgement by adapting their quest for freedom, a game in which the rules were set by white people.

Mary's father was a soldier and a Scotsman. While in Kingston, he stayed in a boarding house run by her mother, a free local woman of mixed black and white parents. She was, according to Jane Robinson, 'probably a mulatto which would make Mary technically a quadroon'.[8]

Mary was always proud of her complexion – and the fairer one was, the greater the advantages, as we shall see later. Mary's mother, Mrs Grant, was an admirable traditional healer of high repute amongst the officers and soldiers of both the army and navy who were stationed at Kingston and their wives. In the 1780s, the islands in the West Indies enjoyed an economic boom, during which vast fortunes were made. The chief source of this wealth was sugar, but there were other smaller valuable crops like coffee and indigo. No wonder, then, that in 1789 one-fifth of Britain's foreign trade was with the British West Indies, and by the 1790s it had increased to one-third. By the late 1790s, the region was responsible for four-fifths of British overseas capital investments and provided over one-eighth of the government's £31.5 million total net revenue through direct taxes and duties. Not surprisingly, to protect British vested interests, large naval and military forces were deployed to the Caribbean. With so much at stake, Britain took no chances with rivals; with a superior force at its command, Britain also colonised new territories. In such operations, Britain was more successful with the smaller islands than the larger ones. Nonetheless, the sheer scale of Britain's presence and power was impressive. Dozens of regiments served in the West Indies. Between 1793 and 1801, 'some 69 line infantry regiments were sent there. Another 24 followed between 1803 and 1815.'[9]

It was to her father that Mary attributed her 'affection for a camp life' and her sympathy for 'the pomp, pride and circumstances of glorious war'.[10] She seemed fascinated by war from an early age. It is clear that she was close to her father, a man of the times, a man of action and principle. She was inclined to believe that the Scottish blood in her veins was responsible for her incredibly high levels of energy and activity, which she said were not always to be found in Creoles. It was this that had impelled her towards a life characterised by variety. To her, the thought of doing one thing for too long was a dismal prospect. The term 'lazy Creole' was a well-known negative reference to Jamaicans (and black people generally) at the time. But this was a stereotype from which she distanced herself. She was different, very much so, and determined to prove her worth. She was unwilling to be tainted by the accusation of indolence. It is significant that early in her life she was aware of a restless energy within, an impulse that kept her on the move and never idle. It was almost second nature for her to be active. 'I have never wanted inclination to rove,' she wrote, 'nor will powerful enough to find a way to carry out my wishes,' – qualities that led her to many countries and brought her 'into some strange and amusing adventures'.[11]

Mrs Grant ran a hotel called Blundell Hall, where British sailors and soldiers who were stationed in the nearby camp, Up-Park, or the military station at Newcastle, met, socialised and convalesced. Soon, through keen interest and hard work, Mary's mother gained a well-deserved reputation. Notable among her successes as a competent 'doctress' was the use of herbal remedies to help the victims of tropical maladies and general sickness.[12] The death rate among British troops due to tropical disease was very high. According to one account:

[From 1793 to 1802] an estimated 45,000 British soldiers died in the West Indies, including about 1,500 officers, nearly all from fevers. In 1796 alone some 41 per cent of the white soldiers died, most of them having arrived within the past year. In the following years, efforts were made to keep white troops out of unhealthy garrisons. As a result, the mortality rate dropped to 15 per cent in 1800 and remained at about 14 per cent from 1803 to 1815. Nevertheless, about 20,000 men died from fevers, including 500 officers.[13]

Mrs Grant's herbal remedies proved to be effective

treatments. About the time that she was a practitioner of the herbal medical art, Thomas Dancer was convinced of the value of Jamaican local medicine and wrote in his book *The Medical Assistant* that 'many of the Simples of [this] Country are endued with considerable efficacy and may be substituted for the Official ones'.[14] Mary's mother was therefore an important person in Kingston who attended to the European officers and men at her lodging house. Much earlier, in 1780, herbal medicines had been applied to cure Britain's greatest hero of the time, Lord Nelson, of dysentery.[15]

Mary was not her parents' only child. She had a brother, Edward, and a sister, Louisa. Her early life was very interesting and very unusual for a non-white child in colonial Jamaica, especially in the time of slavery. Her mother was very close and attentive to her, and naturally Mary followed, insofar as she could, in her mother's footsteps. But in spite of this closeness between mother and daughter, there was another woman with whom she spent a good deal of time during her childhood. According to Mary, this person was an old lady who treated her as one of her own grandchildren. Nonetheless, the woman's concern and kindness were 'no replacement' for Mary's mother. But, even being aware of this, Mary recognised that she was so spoiled by the old lady that, were it not for seeing her mother and her patients as often as she did, Mary thought it very likely that she would have grown up 'idle and useless'. Clearly she was highly valued, which boosted her self-esteem.

Not surprisingly, Mary was imbued with a sense of self, and from about the age of twelve she was spending more time at home with her mother and would assist with household duties. Often, she would confide in her mother 'the ambition to become a doctress' which 'took firm root in my mind'. She admitted to being very young and lacking knowledge, but what little she had was gained by observing her mother. The propensity for children to play-act (and Mary was no exception) led her to relate how readily she imposed her 'childish griefs and blandishments' upon a doll. Quick learner that she was, Mary made 'good use' of her 'dumb companion and confidante'. Thus, her doll was susceptible to every disease that affected the local people, and her fertile, growing mind imagined medical triumphs that resulted in saving a few 'valuable lives'. None of these simulations, however, were as gratifying as fancying the 'glow of health' returning to the doll's face after long and life-threatening illnesses. As ambition got the better of Mary, she was sufficiently in the habit of empathy and sympathy to extend her practice to 'dogs and cats' to whom she transferred their owners' diseases. In turn, she would administer the likely remedies she deemed suitable for the complaints. In time, her ministrations grew more ambitious, and in the absence of human patients she would play out the patient/nurse roles herself.[16]

The sea was always close by as Mary grew up. Kingston Harbour was crowded with ships of various shapes and sizes. And, having been lively and ambitious from an early age, Mary was smitten by a longing to travel. Her imagination ranged freely as she traced her finger over an old map, moving it along and up from island to island in the Caribbean Sea and then across the Atlantic from Jamaica to England. She was fond of the 'stately ships' in Kingston Harbour, many of them bound for England. Soon her improbable, girlish longing was realised, for, as she put it, 'circumstances, which I need not explain, enabled me to accompany some relatives to England while I was yet a very young woman.'[17] How young? A relatively recent biography dates this first visit to England to 1822, when Mary was about nineteen years old.[18] Once again, this raises interesting questions. For example, who were her 'relatives'? Mary wrote that her companion was 'very dark', but it is worth speculating whether a white person was also travelling with them. Slavery was the defining factor in colonial life at this time. Yet Mary mentions little or nothing about it in Jamaica, and from the tone of her writing, in retrospect, she seemed little bothered or affected by that 'peculiar institution'. She was eager, though, to expand on her first impressions of the great metropolis, London. It is significant that she came into contact with street boys who made fun of her colour. In England this was especially interesting to Mary, who was like an island – a conspicuous minority surrounded by a sea of white. She became acutely self-conscious. Her skin was different, even though it was 'only a little brown', which she regarded as nearly white.[19]

In the 1820s, there were many black people in and around Central London, although the black population had dwindled to an estimated 10,000 from 15,000 in the 1780s.[20] The anti-slavery movement and parliamentary reform were key issues in London. Thus far in her life, references to Mary's complexion may have mattered much less than they did now that she was surrounded by the white multitudes of London. If it had not happened before, it was here and now that an awareness of her skin colour would burn itself into her consciousness. For now, the street boys reminded her at every turn of this aspect of her presence. But although Mary writes little or nothing about the matter, it would be very surprising if she did not encounter people in London who were much darker in complexion than she was. Generations of black people had lived there, and now the evidence was to be seen in their descendants. Indeed, around this time, the young and soon-to-be-famous black Chartist William Cuffay was playing his part in the Chartist campaign for economic and social justice. Years later, at the time of the delivery of the People's Charter to Parliament, he was charged, convicted and transported to Tasmania, where he spent the rest of his days in a workhouse.[21] So parliamentary reform, Chartism and anti-slavery were issues that all contributed to a raised awareness of the question of race and freedom among people whose skin was of a darker hue. On these issues Mary remained silent, but to the matter of her race she would return again some years later:

I am only a little brown – a few shades duskier than the brunettes whom you all admire so much; but my companion was very dark, and a fair (if I can apply the term to her) subject for their rude wit. She was hot-tempered, poor thing! And as there were no policemen to awe the boys and turn our servants' head in those days, our progress through the London streets was sometimes a rather chequered one.[22]

We do not know where Mary stayed for the year she spent in England before returning to Kingston. But soon she was on her way back, making her second trip to London. This visit was, for the curious young woman, an eye-opener. But why did she return so quickly and without a companion? What was it that had lured her? She had observed the trading and commercial focus of the metropolis, which seemed to have enlivened the already burgeoning business sense she had learnt from her mother. Of an astute but caring nature, she quickly recognised opportunities and took them. For her, there were no half-measures; only the maximisation of profits counted. She took a large stock of West Indian preserves and pickles with her to be sold in England, having clearly seen the potential market for all things West Indian. Consumer demand was overwhelming. There was no mistaking the market for her goods in England, that nation of shopkeepers. Thus, on this second visit, she remained in London for two years.

Her return voyage to Jamaica proved to be more adventurous than she had anticipated. It was a trip which very nearly ended in disaster when fire broke out aboard the *Velusia*, the ship on which she was travelling. The cheerful glow of Christmas Eve merriment had rapidly changed to great alarm by Boxing Day. Fortunately for Mary and her fellow passengers, the fire did not spread, and no one was killed. Nonetheless, it was a testing time for all concerned. But amidst the turmoil, the panic among the passengers and the forbidding expanse of the high seas, Mary held her nerve. 'I did not lose my senses', she wrote years later, but admitted that, during the time when the 'contest between fire and water was doubtful', she was pressed to take heed of her own safety and entered into 'an amicable arrangement with the ship's cook, whereby, in consideration of two pounds – which I was not however, to pay until the crisis arrived – he agreed to lash me on to a large hen-coop'.[23]

The average non-stop voyage time across the Atlantic was between eight and ten days, and on her eventual arrival in Kingston Harbour Mary was glad to step on dry land once more. But danger had not dampened her interest in travel. Soon, her wanderlust amplified and propelled her out of Jamaica once more. After a spell on the Caribbean island of New Providence (where she collected shells which she later sold in Kingston), she also visited Haiti and Cuba, islands to which few people of colour had gone as visitors.

Back in Kingston, and now in her early twenties, Mary was as industrious as ever, but found time to visit and nurse her 'old indulgent patroness', who had been ill. Shortly after the lady died, Mary returned to her mother's house, where she made herself useful in a variety of ways, which included learning a great deal more of the Creole medical art.

It was at this time that a Mr Seacole appeared on the scene. Was he a dashing heroic soldier? Mary's descriptions seem to imply the opposite. We know that the man who had entered Mary's life was Edwin Horatio Hamilton Seacole, but we know not where they first met. The Englishman's name seems to suggest some possible connection to Lord Horatio Nelson, the great English hero, and his mistress Emma Hamilton. There is not much hard evidence to verify such a link, although attempts have been made.[24] Mary said little or nothing about her betrothal to Edwin Seacole. She may have been too busy, and could well not have been the sort to wallow or engage in prolonged courtship. What she did say about this man who had come into her life was that after he had timidly proposed to her, they were married. If their engagement was brief, their honeymoon was perhaps even briefer, for soon enough they had established a provisions store in Black River on Jamaica's south-west coast. Since her childhood, and now as a vigorous young woman, she was engaged in a punishing schedule of errands and activities to do with her parents' business and with caring of one sort or another.

Because of her parents' close ties with the army and doctors, Mary gained invaluable knowledge and experience which she later combined with the folk medicine learnt from her mother.[25] Now, as a wife, Mary combined her nursing activities with business. In time, her reputation as a 'doctress' surpassed that of her mother. She was now able to deal effectively with diseases that frequently struck down and killed Jamaicans, such as cholera, yellow fever, malaria and smallpox.

Then, much too soon, she had to come to terms with losing her ailing husband. After they had established their store in Black River, Mary realised how ill Edwin had become:

> Poor man! he was very delicate and before I undertook the charge of him, several doctors had expressed most unfavourable opinions of his health. I kept him alive by kind nursing and attention as long as I could; but at last he grew so ill that we left Black River [...][26]

She returned to her mother's home in Kingston and a few weeks later Edwin died. His passing marked a shift in mood, unlike anything Mary had hitherto experienced. It was a bitter blow, her 'first great trouble', which touched her deeply:

> For days I never stirred – lost to all that passed around me in a stupor of despair. If you had told me that the

time would soon come when I should remember this sorrow calmly, I should not have believed it possible: and yet it was so.[27]

With the accumulation of knowledge and wisdom, she contemplated her response as a Creole to such a moment in life. 'I do not think that we hot-blooded Creoles sorrow less for showing it so impetuously,' she explained, 'but I do think that the sharp edge of our grief wears down sooner than theirs who preserve an outward appearance of calmness, and nurse their woe secretly in their hearts.'[28]

2

Business and Nursing

In the wake of Edwin's death and Mary's mourning, Mary's dear mother also passed away. Mary was now alone in the world, battling as best she could. But just when it seemed all was lost, the trying struggles that followed taught her invaluable lessons about the cost of success in life. Later she would reflect upon having 'turned a bold front to fortune'. Her life as a widow was not only lonely but also financially difficult. In spite of setbacks, she never allowed herself to succumb to despair or depression and, as a result, she succeeded in gaining not only a living but many comforts besides. But even then, her experience of the world led her to conclude that it was 'by no means the hard bad world which some selfish people would have us believe'.[1]

Whatever Mary was, it was clear to everyone that she was not selfish.[2] Her optimism was integral to her warm, caring nature. Among other positive characteristics, she was hearty, strong and plain-spoken. She was enterprising and steady enough, maintaining her composure as her fortunes rose and fell. By her own admission, she never thought only of making money. She believed 'that we were born to be happy, and that the surest way to be wretched is to prize it [money] overmuch'.[3] This contrasts, to some extent, with other accounts, one in particular, which tended to over-emphasise her profit-making zeal at the expense of her humanitarian concern. Even if the case against her profiteering was not true, she put money in proper perspective thus:

> Had I [overly prized money], I should have mourned over many a promising speculation proving a failure, over many a pan of preserves or guava jelly burnt in the making; and perhaps lost my mind when the great fire of 1843, which devastated Kingston, burnt down my poor home. As it was, I very nearly lost my life, for I would not leave my house until every chance of saving it had gone, and it was wrapped in flames. But, of course, I set to work again in a humbler way, and rebuilt my house by degrees, and restocked it, succeeding better than before [...][4]

At the age of 38, pragmatic and full of common sense might be a good description of Mary Seacole.

Why did she succeed better than before? In part, because the environment was conducive. She knew well the limitations under which she operated, but she exploited the space of being a free woman of colour, constantly hustling, seeking opportunities and making the most of them when they arose. Her goodness of heart, caring ways and close observation of her mother and others had, by now, gained for her a reputation as a skilful nurse and 'doctress', which was tested by visits to her home by invalid British officers and their wives, and occasionally a naval or military surgeon. Mary learned a great deal from these educated men as she practised her medical art.

Although Mary had many acquaintances, including friends of her former husband, it seems she had no romantic liaison, a state of being which was through choice. She was confident enough in her own powers, and it was not from necessity that she stayed an unprotected female. If anything, one of the hardest struggles of her life at this time was to resist men who pressed her to marry them. She leaves us in no doubt as to what she felt about marriage at this time: clearly, she was not preoccupied by this institution. Of greater value to her was the presence of officers of all ranks who were guests in her boarding house. More and more, her reputation grew and she became well known among the soldiers who visited Jamaica. The wounded and ailing respected her as a motherly figure. And with her Scottish background, her house was an especially welcoming 'home from home' for the British soldiers. Americans were also regular visitors, and business, it seems, ran smoothly.

Then, in 1850, when Mary was 45 years old, Jamaica was struck by cholera. The origin of the outbreak, in her view, was in the garments of an infected person who had travelled on a steamer from New Orleans. While the disease spread, one of her lodgers, a doctor, took a keen interest in knowing what treatment was required. Naturally, Mary took note. The knowledge she gained was invaluable.

That same year, her brother, Edward, had left Kingston for the Isthmus of Panama, described by Mary as the 'high-road to and from golden California', where he had established a considerable store and hotel.[5] She found his lead irresistible – all the more so as visitors came and went, leaving her with their exciting stories. An additional reason for her to make the journey to Chagres, on the isthmus, was her brother's weak constitution. Once the decision was made, she placed her house in the hands of a cousin and made garments such as coats, trousers and shirts, and foodstuffs – preserves, guava jelly and other delicacies, also preserved meats, vegetables and eggs – which she felt sure her brother would need. With this baggage, she travelled to Panama. Thus the urge to roam (her father's influence) was accompanied by the prospects of nursing and the selling (her mother's influence) of much-needed foodstuffs.

Her journey across the isthmus was short. But while it was 'insignificant' in distance, it was by no means 'an easy one'.[6] On either side of this land mass were the two great oceans, the Atlantic and Pacific. If Mary was in awe of them, she was hardly impressed by life in the isthmus, where the lack of civilisation struck her powerfully. How unlike colonial Jamaica it was. She was not impressed. Chagres and wider Panama were appalling places, and the California Gold Rush did little to make them more attractive. It was a time when thousands of people were crossing the isthmus to reach the west coast of the United States. A combination of poverty, disease and lawlessness blighted the region. The more mature Mrs Seacole, the widowed businesswoman, was trying to make a living in a dirt town with little or no prospects. Not surprisingly, she moved on. The steamer she travelled on went on to Navy Bay, which was hardly an improvement on the place she had just left. She described it as a 'luckless, dreary spot', swampland in which the houses were built upon piles. For the health-conscious Mary, this was a dangerous environment. Her concern that it was a nursery for ague, fever and eventually death was echoed by many who had travelled there with her. This potential for disease made Mary keen to speed ahead to reach her brother, but it also ignited her humanitarian concern and a desire to help the victims of disease that had overrun Navy Bay. Although her stay there was short – just one night – it was enough to call her medicine chest into requisition. Sadly, what the sick wanted were remedies she could not give: warmth, nourishment and fresh air. The scene she beheld was that of men dying from sheer exhaustion.

From here, Mary began her journey towards Cruces. The first stage was by railway to Gatun, some twelve miles away. En route, she noted that unhealthy stretches of countryside gave way to glimpses of hills in the distance that were reminiscent of the English countryside.[7] The true cost of the railway on which she travelled was, however, thousands of lives. The line ended at Gatun, and she travelled on via the River Chagres to Gorgona before journeying on to the town of Cruces, where her brother lived and worked. As previously, she said little or nothing about her sister, Louisa. At this stage, although Mary's self-possession, her independence of mind, had become more pronounced, it is important to note that she did not travel alone. She was accompanied by her assistants: a black servant called Mac and a little girl. They not only kept her company but may also have afforded her, as a lone female traveller, much-needed protection in some quite outlandish places.

One of the significant lessons for Mary on this journey from Jamaica to Cruces was the knowledge that there were 'two species' of individuals whom she found to be the same wherever she went: porters and lawyers. Her unsatisfactory dealings with these men were compounded by other problems, such as the loss of several articles from her luggage. The fact that she had hired her own boat gives a clear indication of her energy, drive and resourcefulness. She could not be fobbed off easily. If her path were blocked, she would look for another route, which says much for her inventiveness.

On her travels, Mary was reminded of, and came to learn more about, her race. Did she have a problem with this? Years later, she explained herself thus:

I think, if I have a little prejudice against our cousins across the Atlantic – and I do confess to a little – it is not unreasonable. I have a few shades of deeper brown upon my skin which shows me related – and I am proud of the relationship – to those poor mortals whom you once held enslaved, and whose bodies America still owns. And having this bond, and knowing what slavery is; having seen with my eyes and heard with my ears proof positive enough of its horrors – let others affect to doubt them if they will – is it surprising that I should be somewhat impatient of the airs of superiority which many Americans have endeavoured to assume over me?[8]

With renewed determination, she eventually succeeded in hiring a boat which took her on the last leg to Cruces. Although travel excited her, its wear and tear took its toll. She disembarked tired, wretched and out of temper.

On arrival in Cruces, Mary looked forward to staying at her brother's Independent Hotel, which she hoped could not fail to be acceptable, especially after a long night on the wretched boat. And sure enough, when they met, Edward had the kindest welcome in his face. But, as he led the way to his house, disillusionment was not long in coming. Mary surveyed the street and its surroundings as they walked and was surprised by what she found. 'I was miserably unprepared for the reception that awaited me,' she recalled.[9] Amidst the dampness, dirt and confusion, a crowd of gold-diggers had encamped. Stiff, cold and hungry, when she eventually reached her destination, she was disappointed to find that the Independent Hotel was a miserable-looking long, low hut, built of rough, unhewn, unplaned logs filled up with mud. Apart from the lack of space and privacy, she speculated that guests engaging in orgies was not out of the question, and rest, warmth and comfort were miserable delusions. By now, she had run out of patience with her brother: 'What am I to do? Why did you ever bring me to this place? See what a state I am in – cold, hungry and wretched. I want to wash, to change my clothes, to eat [...]'[10]

Mary's questions and complaints were met with a shake of the head and a shrug of the shoulders by Edward. She realised it was a strange life she had come to and, for a while, attributed her troubles to the novelty of her position. But a change here was not as good as a rest. She watched the visitors come and go, especially passengers on their way to and from California. Gold-digging was clearly on their minds, but Mary soon found out that a prized objective of all the travellers was dinner or supper. In addition, wine and spirits were available but, according to Mary, the Americans seldom partook.

Gambling, which somehow seemed linked to gold prospecting, was not allowed in Edward's hotel. There was an expectant feverish excitement among travellers and prospectors, but for travel-weary Mary, rest was uppermost in her mind. She needed a bed, but all rooms were taken. In exasperation, she pinned an oilskin tablecloth around the legs of a long table to create a makeshift four-poster bed canopy. Eventually, as she lay on the floor underneath the table, together with her servant girl, tiredness and sleep overtook her.

In her wandering life, it was helpful that Mary was now in Cruces, where she declared that she had never known 'what it is to despair or even to despond'.[11] Did this mean that a night's rest had so invigorated her that she could face anything? More accurately, perhaps, she was blessed with an unusually strong physical constitution. Where others were lethargic, she exuded robustness. She recognised and welcomed the 'bright side' of life in the town and became involved in local schemes. Ever ambitious, she aspired to open her own hotel, but for now she was prepared to bide her time by putting up at her brother's house. Soon, cholera broke out in Cruces and local people laid the blame for the disease on a traveller from New Orleans, a port that seemed to harbour carriers. Predictably, Mary was ready and willing to help. In fact, she was so prepared that one wonders whether she was expecting it. She was conscious of her surroundings, a keen and astute observer. In later life she explained, 'There was no doctor in Cruces; the nearest approach to one was a little timid dentist, who was there by accident and who refused to prescribe for the sufferer, and I was obliged to do my best.' With her medicine kit, which she carried on her travels, she was usually the first on the scene. In Cruces she hurried to the first patient and applied the appropriate remedies. She described this case as 'very obstinate' and wrote, 'by dint of mustard emetics, warm fomentations, mustard plasters on the stomach and the back, and calomel, at first in large then in gradually smaller doses, I succeeded in saving my first cholera patient in Cruces.'[12] The hope of local people that the disease would eventually pass away after a few days was a false one. With frightful suddenness, the cholera spread rapidly, and Mary was so fully employed that she scarcely had much rest. But, far from complaining, she was surprised by the calamity and her response to it:

> I do not deny (it is the only thing indeed that I have to be proud of) that I am pleased and gratified when I look upon my past life, and see times now and then, and places here and there, when and where I have been enabled to benefit my fellow creatures suffering from ills my skill could often remedy.[13]

Quick and willing learner that she was, Mary soon realised the power of the disease. There was little fight among those affected, she noted: the people's 'slavish despair' before the plague is how Mary put it. There was not even 'the feeblest show of resistance'. Invoking the saints with 'passionate prayers and cries' was not enough.[14] The environment was not conducive to fighting disease. She was not religious, being instead pragmatic and brutally honest. Very quickly, it became clear that the people of Cruces needed her:

Very likely the Saints would have got the credit of helping them if they had helped themselves; but the poor cowards never stirred a finger to clean out their close, reeking huts, or rid the damp street of the rotting accumulation of months. I think their chief reliance was on "the yellow woman from Jamaica with the cholera medicine".[15]

This did not surprise Mary, 'because the Spanish doctor, who was sent for from Panama [...] was unfamiliar with the terrible disease he was called upon to do battle with'.[16]

Mary received adequate pay for her services from those few who were well-off, but she had to be content with thanks from the impoverished majority. Unpleasant a task as it was, she preferred working with the American store- and hotelkeeper, rather than the boatmen and muleteers, who suffered terrible losses in scenes of horror that were unforgettable. As the plague claimed more lives, the demands on Mary's time increased. She had little time to think. Her attention to the sick and dying was total. Then she was confronted with a major decision following the death of a one-year-old child. Her powerlessness to save the infant provoked in her a new approach to dealing with cholera. With the child's lifeless body in her arms, she thought of a novel idea. Put simply, she felt she could learn from the child's death. The time had come to be bold in thought and action. If she could examine the dead child, she thought, she could learn a great deal about the disease which showed no sign of petering out. The situation was desperate; there was no time to lose. Her mind was made up. She felt justified in taking the step she had intended: 'I knew the fled spirit would not reproach me, for I had done all I could for it in life – had shed tears over it, and prayed for it.'[17] Now, on a cold grey morning, as the child was taken away for burial, Mary followed the man who carried the body. She bribed the man to take a lonely path that led to the riverside. They both stopped at a bushy part of the riverbank, and Mary persuaded the man to assist her in performing her first and last post-mortem examination. It was, to say the least, a courageous act, an extraordinary initiative on Mary's part, and the results were 'decidedly useful', she recalled in later years. Though medical men were already familiar with the kind of thing that she had done in secrecy, the knowledge she had gained bolstered her confidence as a nurse and 'doctress'.[18]

After burying the child, Mary and her accomplice slipped back into Cruces like guilty criminals. But the silver experiment yielded a golden pay-off, for the knowledge she had gained was invaluable to her. She applied herself to her practice and was now more confident that she knew which medicines worked and which did not. She confirmed this some years later, when she wrote that the simplest remedies were perhaps the best: 'Mustard plasters, and emetics, and calomel; the mercury applied externally, where the veins were nearest the surface, were my usual resources.'[19] She dreaded opium, and to thirsty patients she gave water 'in which cinnamon had been boiled. Above all, I never neglected to apply mustard poultices to the stomach, spine, and neck, and particularly to keep my patient warm about the region of the heart.'[20] Qualified medical doctors may have treated these patients differently, but persistent care after the disease had passed was Mary's approach. What did she learn from all this? The 'great conclusion' which her practice among cholera sufferers had brought her to was 'the old one that few constitutions permitted the use of exactly similar remedies and that the course of treatment which saved one man, would, if persisted in, have very likely killed his brother'.[21]

Throughout the epidemic her presence was required here, there and everywhere. She willingly sacrificed herself to the care of others, and in so doing she was exposed to the disease. One day, she realised her own vulnerability when symptoms of cholera showed themselves in her. Not knowing to whom she should turn, she hurried to her brother's house. There she experienced a frightening moment, when an unpleasant chill overtook her and she was forced to go to bed. Other symptoms followed. Before nightfall, she had become a victim of the dreaded cholera, which had attacked 'perhaps its greatest foe in Cruces'.[22]

This was a cruel blow for Mary. News that she was afflicted spread fast. And when the people of Cruces heard, they were magnanimous in showing their gratitude, concern and sympathy for the woman they called the 'Yellow Doctress'. While Mary was grateful, the attention that she received had its downside. Being ill was, for Mary, a rare experience, which deepened her understanding:

> Indeed, when I most wanted quiet, it was difficult to keep out the sympathising Americans and sorrowing natives who came to inquire after me; and who, not content with making their inquiries, and leaving their offerings of blankets, flannel, etc., must see with their own eyes what chance the yellow woman had of recovery. The rickety door of my little room could never be kept shut for many minutes together. A visitor would open it silently, poke his long face in with an expression of sympathy that almost made me laugh in spite of my pain, draw it out again, between the narrowest possible opening, as if he were anxious to admit as little air as he could; while another would come in bodily, and after looking at me curiously and inquisitively, as he would eye a horse or [enslaved black person] he had some thoughts of making a bid for, would help to carpet my room, with the result perhaps of his meditations, and saying, gravely, "Air you better, Aunty Seacole, now? Isn't there a something we can du for you, ma'am?" would as gravely give place to another and another yet, until I was almost inclined to throw something at them, and call them bad names, like the Scotch King does the ghosts in the play.[23]

Fortunately, Mary had only a mild attack of cholera, though for a while she felt 'weak and exhausted'. It was the local population's good fortune that a few weeks later there were no more new cases of the disease, and it eventually stopped. Thereafter, the survivors of Cruces pursued life with characteristic briskness and selfishness, as the horrors of the cholera faded.

With her reputation enhanced, there was much in store for Mary. The Americans who ran the place retained her services as their 'medical attendant'. While this post kept her as busy as possible, it did not deflect her attention from pursuing her original purpose of running a hotel in Cruces. Her medical work and her ambition as a hotelier seemed to bring balance to her life, which she welcomed. This quest for centredness, for balance, would recur time and again in Mary's life. At last, she found a building which she hoped to transform into her hotel. Now economic considerations preoccupied her. Though the monthly rent of £20 was 'fair', there was room for improvement. Eventually, the building which she regarded as a 'tumbledown hut' was refurbished with a variety of trimmings including calico of bright colours, fringes, frills and bows, which gave much pleasure to the Americans. She was determined to keep lodgers out, running the place solely as an eating house. Her staff included Mac, her black servant; her servant girl; and a local cook. Whatever she had learnt from her brother about the hotel business, headstrong Mary ultimately fixed her own charges. She explained, 'For an ordinary dinner my charge was four shillings; eggs and chickens were [...] distinct luxuries, and fetched high prices.'[24]

In those early days, the majority of her clients were on their way to California, and Mary described them as 'rough, rude men, of dirty, quarrelsome habits'.[25] But she regarded those few who were more civilised as being more dangerous. It was therefore no surprise that before long she grew very tired of life in Cruces, even though she made money quickly. But thoughts of leaving also moved her to press her brother to return to Kingston.

While managing her hotel in Cruces, Mary realised once more how unprotected she was as a woman. At times, she was faced with the difficult task of managing rowdy travellers and guests. The coarse females and the dinner habits of many Americans were of special interest to Mary, who observed:

Very often quarrels would arise during the progress of dinner; and more than once I thought the knives, which they nearly swallowed at every mouthful, would have been turned against one another. It was, I always thought, extremely fortunate that the reckless men rarely stimulated their excitable passions with strong drink. Tea and coffee were the common beverages of the Americans; Englishmen, and men of other nations, being generally distinguishable by their demand for wine and spirits. But the Yankee's capacity for swilling tea and coffee was prodigious. I saw one man drink ten cups of coffee; and finding his appetite still unsatisfied, I ran across to my brother for advice. There was a merry twinkle in his eyes as he whispered, "I always put in a good spoonful of salt after the sixth cup. It chokes them off admirably."[26]

Theft and cheating were endemic among unscrupulous travellers. And once again, it was 'only the 'cutest Yankee who stood any fair chance of outwitting' the vigilant Mary.[27] She learned fast about the business as the challenges confronted her. For example, gambling was a business that accrued the primary reward of money made from the gold-seekers, yet no one cared enough to make gambling houses look attractive. Occasionally, however, a few 'distinguished' travellers passed her way. One of them, Mary wrote in her autobiography, was the dancer and actress Lola Montez, who was bound for California; another was Catherine Hayes, the singer. But Mary's reference to Montez is problematic, for, as one writer states, the dancer was never in Cruces.[28]

The problem that confronted Mary was that the majority of the crowds were very rowdy. They tended to devalue life, and were ready on a whim to kill or be killed over the slightest provocation. The intimidating nature of a crowd's arrival or departure always contained potentially violent elements. The noise they made was loud. Their behaviour was raucous. But even this could not deflect Mary's attention away from an aspect of life in Cruces that commanded her attention. She wrote:

Against the Negroes, of whom there were many in the Isthmus, and who almost invariably filled the municipal offices, and took the lead in every way, the Yankees had a strong prejudice; but it was wonderful to see how freedom and equality elevate man, and the same Negro who perhaps in Tennessee would have cowered like a beaten child or dog beneath an American's uplifted hand, would face him boldly here, and by equal courage and superior physical strength cow his old oppressor.[29]

By now, Mary had come to know the local community well enough to treat elements of it with due caution. Time and again, certain themes emerged: crime and punishment, law and order. Thieving was prevalent, although Mary was careful to state that black people did not participate in this practised and skilful activity. An honest day's work for an honest day's pay was not a given in Cruces, even though punishments were quite severe. In this lawless place, Mary's approach to justice was simple: she did not rely on the law for protection, for ultimately it was an expensive luxury. She cited Americans as being the group that was hardest to bring to justice. Put simply, some got away with murder.

It was at the end of the rainy season that Mary prepared to leave Cruces for Gorgona. But before doing so, it was customary for store- and hotelkeepers to exchange visits and attend each other's parties. Mary's popularity in the community had grown, partly because of her medical contribution during the cholera crisis. Of the many invitations she received, the most important was held on American Independence Day at her brother's hotel, where high-spirited Americans dined. Much champagne was drunk, and after patriotic toasts attention was focused on Mary, whose keen ear picked up what was said at the time. The speaker was a 'thin, sallow-looking American' who spoke rapidly. Mary reported his words:

Well, gentlemen, I expect you'll all support me in a drinking of this toast that I du—. Aunty Seacole, gentlemen; I give you, Aunty Seacole—. We can't du less for her, after what she's done for us—, when the cholera was among us, gentlemen—, not many months ago—. So, I say, God bless the best yaller woman He ever made—, from Jamaica, gentlemen—, from the Isle of Springs— Well, gentlemen, I expect there are only tu things we're vexed for—; and the first is, that she ain't one of us—, a citizen of the great United States—; and the other thing is, gentlemen—, that Providence made her a yaller woman. I calculate, gentlemen, you're all as vexed as I am that she's not wholly white—, but I du reckon on your rejoicing with me that she's so many shades removed from being entirely black—; and I guess, if we could bleach her by any means we would—, and thus make her as acceptable in any company as she deserves to be—. Gentlemen, I give you Aunty Seacole![30]

The speaker was applauded, but Mary was not amused. Incensed by the reference to her race, although her brother cautioned her not to speak too freely, she said:

> Gentlemen – I return you my best thanks for your kindness in drinking my health. As for what I have done in Cruces, Providence evidently made me to be useful, and I can't help it. But, I must say, that I don't altogether appreciate your friend's kind wishes with respect to my complexion. If it had been as dark as any [black person]'s, I should have been just as happy and as useful, and as much respected by those whose respect I value; and as to his offer of bleaching me, I should, even if it were practicable, decline it without any thanks. As to the society which the process might gain me admission into, all I can say is, that, judging from the specimens I have met with here and elsewhere, I don't think that I shall lose much by being excluded from it. So, gentlemen, I drink to you and the general reformation of American manners.[31]

The sense of herself and how others viewed her aroused strong responses from Mary. She did not think her speech was well received, believing that although the Americans laughed 'good naturedly', it was because she was 'a somewhat privileged person'.[32] This hypocrisy was not to her liking, for she would have much preferred it if they had been angry.

With her mind set on moving on to Gorgona, although business was very much on her mind, Mary was concerned about leaving behind her brother, who was young and prone to illness. In Gorgona, Mary's business as a hotelier was uppermost in her mind. When, at last, she found a 'miserable little hut' for sale and bought it for $100, she set about renovating it. The accommodation here was, in some respects, superior to her previous property. Here, she was willing to try something different. She decided to provide the public, her customers, with an unusual, almost exclusive service. Her establishment would be open, in large part, to entertain 'ladies' and those in need of care and attention. In the meantime, she persisted in trying to influence her brother. But in spite of her best efforts to persuade him to leave the Isthmus of Panama, he was determined to stay. She began to have serious thoughts about leaving him there.

At this time, there were also gaps in Mary's life that she felt needed to be filled. The limitations were obvious, she thought. She needed to explore, to move on. But she was careful to state that it was not 'altogether my old roving inclination which led me to desire a change'; it was also that she did not think her present life was 'agreeable for a woman with the least delicacy or refinement; and of female society I had none.'[33] And yet she was prone to avoid the women that came her way. She found many of them to be either bad or disagreeable, and she had special difficulty dealing with most women from the southern states of America:

[Those southern women] showed an instinctive repugnance against any one whose countenance claimed for her kindred with their slaves, [so] my position was far from a pleasant one. Not that it ever gave me any annoyance; they were glad of my stores and comforts, I made money out of their wants; nor do I think our bond of connection was ever closer.[34]

But even if this caused her no annoyance, she leaves us in no doubt of her magnanimity when she states that 'if any of them came to me sick and suffering (I say this out of simple justice to myself), I forgot everything, except that she was my sister, and that it was my duty to help her'.[35]

In Gorgona as in Cruces, Mary reflected, the likelihood of flooding was real. Although her hotel was on higher ground, she was nonetheless known to have suffered 'some distressing losses'. Then, when fire ravaged Gorgona, Mary had had enough. Leaving her hotel in her brother's hands, she prepared to return to Kingston.

But leaving the calamities of this place to return home was not the end of her discomfiture or distress, for a hitherto new experience awaited her at the Navy Bay quayside. She was anxious to get home and had booked her passage on the first steamer, which was American-owned. Late in the evening of her departure, she bade farewell to friends with whom she had been staying and boarded the steamer. One of her very kind friends, an American merchant, approached her with the advice that she should 'delay' her

journey until an English steamer was available. This struck
Mary as being odd, all the more because the American
friend could not give a good reason for delaying her trip.
And so without further delay Mary proceeded with Mac
and her little maid to pass through a crowd of female passengers on her way to the saloon. After a short while, two
women came up and questioned her:

"Where air you going?"
"To Kingston."
"And how air you going?"
"By sea."
"Don't be impertinent, yaller woman. By what con-
veyance air you going?"
"By this steamer, of course. I've paid for my passage."[36]

Mary kept calm as the women went away, in the full
knowledge that she had paid for her passage. This was the
end of the matter as far as she was concerned. But soon
she was surrounded by eight or nine white women who
repeated the questions about her destination and how
she was going to get there. Mary's answers raised quite a
storm of uncomplimentary remarks, as she recorded in
her memoir:

"Guess a [racial slur] woman don't go along with us in
this saloon," said one. "I never travelled with a [racial
slur] yet, and I expect I shan't begin now," said another;

while some children had taken my little servant Mary in hand, and were practising on her the politenesses which their parents were favouring me with – only, as is the wont of children, they were crueller. I cannot help it if I shock my readers; but the truth is, that one positively spat in poor little Mary's frightened yellow face.

At last an old American lady came to where I sat, and gave me some staid advice. "Well, now, I tell you for your good, you'd better quit this, and not drive my people to extremities. If you do, you'll be sorry for it, I expect." Thus harassed, I appealed to the stewardess – a tall sour-looking woman, flat and thin as a dressed-up broomstick. She asked me sundry questions as to how and when I had taken my passage; until, tired beyond all endurance, I said, "My good woman, put me anywhere – under a boat – in your store-room, so that I can get to Kingston somehow." But the stewardess was not to be moved.

"There's nowhere but the saloon, and you can't expect to stay with the white people, that's clear. Flesh and blood can stand a good deal of aggravation; but not that. If the Britishers is so took up with coloured people, that's their business; but it won't do here."

This last remark was in answer to an Englishman, whose advice to me was not to leave my seat for any of them. He made matters worse; until at last I lost my temper, and calling Mac, bade him get my things together, and went up to the captain – a good honest man. He and some of the black crew and the black cook, who showed his teeth most viciously, were much annoyed. Muttering about its being a custom of the country, the captain gave me an order upon the agent for the money I had paid; and so, at twelve o'clock at night, I was landed again upon the wharf of Navy Bay.

My American friends were vastly annoyed, but not much surprised; and two days later, the English steamer, the "Eagle," in charge of my old friend, Captain B—, touched at Navy Bay, and carried me to Kingston.[37]

3

Determined to Serve

In 1853, on her return to Jamaica from Panama, Mary found her services were needed because of an outbreak of yellow fever, which had hit the island with such severity that she thought it would destroy the English people on the island. The raging epidemic claimed the lives of many, including some who were close to Mary. In Mary's house, there were many sufferers – officers, wives and children. Fortunately for these victims, Mary was in the right place at the right time. But although she had seen a great deal of suffering and death, she found these Jamaican scenes more difficult to bear than any at which she had previously been present. In the circumstances, she found that as well as trying to lift the spirits of the patients, she also had the difficult task of helping the bereaved:

> It was a terrible thing to see young people in the youth and bloom of life suddenly stricken down, not in battle with an enemy that threatened their country, but in vain contest with a climate that refused to adopt them.

Indeed, the mother country pays a dear price for the possession of her colonies.[1]

Her empathy and sympathy for England and Britishness was not in doubt. Although she would later generalise, it is clear she was referring to herself when she wrote:

> I think all who are familiar with the West Indies will acknowledge that Nature has been favourable to strangers in a few respects, and that one of these has been in instilling into the hearts of the Creoles an affection for English people and an anxiety for their welfare, which shows itself warmest when they are sick and suffering.[2]

Furthermore, she pointed to another benefit that had been conferred upon the English, namely the practice among Creoles of the healing art, which induced them to seek out 'the simple remedies which are available for the terrible diseases by which foreigners are attacked, and which are found growing under the same circumstances which produce the ills they minister to'. She reflected, 'So true is it that beside the nettle ever grows the cure for its sting.'[3]

Thus far, it had been difficult for Mary to avoid human suffering, dying and death. For better or worse, these were the scenes with which she was most familiar. Amidst it all, she was not squeamish but rather forthright in her views on those whom she had now and then accompanied a little distance on their way into the valley of the shadow of death. After many years of caring, she expressed her thoughts on death, a fear of which she said no one need be ashamed. 'How we bear it depends much upon our constitutions,' she believed. As the number of casualties mounted, she considered the brave men who endured 'the cruellest amputation' with a smile, men who died 'trembling like children' and those who drew their last breath 'like heroes'.[4] But, she declared, she would not attribute the peace and resignation she had seen to temperament alone. She was not overly religious, and she expressed her belief thus:

> I have stood by receiving the last blessings of Christians; and closing the eyes of those who had nothing to trust to but the mercy of a God who will be far more merciful to us than we are to one another; and I say decidedly that the Christian's death is the glorious one, as is his life [...] and as the work of the hands earns for us sweet rest by night, so does the heart's labour of a lifetime make the repose of heaven acceptable.[5]

Nonetheless, proximity to death did not make her insensitive to it. In fact, the smell of death was never far away and the passings of some were more memorable than others. She remembered one man's death that touched her deeply. His dying moments taught her that when her time came, she would approach it with a brave, smiling face. This man's demise was the best example of the nobility of dying, Mary argued. She identified him as a young surgeon, who had been kind to her in many ways. When he fell ill, he was taken to her house. As she nursed him, she grew fond of him, so much so that she felt almost as close to him as his mother, who was thousands of miles away in England. The scenes she witnessed were poignant. When the man knew that he would not survive his illness, that death was imminent, he projected a selfless quality which touched Mary. He showed little regard for himself. All his pity, she said, was for those he was leaving behind. Instead of leaving the matter to rest, she dramatised the scene in her autobiography, many years later:

> It was trying to see his poor hands tremblingly penning the last few words of leavetaking – trying to see how piteously the poor worn heart longed to see once more the old familiar faces of the loved ones in unconscious happiness at home.

Mary's feelings were abundant, and she felt they were well received. In the absence of the man's loved ones, she was conscious of her supportive role, and felt her nursing was worthwhile. 'I think he had some fondness for me, or, perhaps, his kind heart feigned a feeling that he saw would give me joy; for I used to call him "my son – my dear child," and to weep over him in a very weak and silly manner perhaps.' [6] But death, as she reflected, was not to be feared, nor was its effect silly. She then described the young man's final moments of life thus: 'He sent for an old friend [...] and when he came, I had to listen to the dictation of his simple will – his dog to one friend, his ring to another, his books to a third, his love and kind wishes to all.' Once this was done, she wrote of her 'poor son':

> [...] he prepared himself to die – a child in all save a man's calm courage. He beckoned me to raise him in the bed, and, as I passed my arms around him, he saw the tears I could not repress, rolling down my brown cheeks, and thanked me with a few words. "Let me lay my head upon your breast;" and so he rested, now and then speaking lowly to himself, "It's only that I miss my mother, but Heaven's will be done." He repeated this many times, until the Heaven he obeyed sent him in its mercy forgetfulness, and his thoughts no longer wandered to his earthly home. I heard glad words feebly uttered as I bent over him – words about "Heaven – rest – rest" – a holy Name many times repeated; and then with a smile and a stronger voice, "Home! Home!" And so in a little while my arms no longer held him.[7]

The beloved Englishman in Mary's care passed away. As a memento she kept a little gold brooch with a lock of his hair in it. This was sent to her by the dead man's mother as a keepsake in appreciation of Mary's kindness to her son.

In this long example of a deathbed scene, we get a sense of how close Mary had already become to the English,

Scottish and Irish soldiers to whom she attended in Jamaica. If anything, the death of the young man had a positive effect on her. She began to see the work before her more clearly. There was a greater, more expansive role for her to play. Thus, when she was called upon by the medical authorities to assist in the recruitment of nurses to be employed at Up-Park Camp, a short distance from Kingston, the dutiful Mary left a few nurses at home and went to do her best to mitigate the severity of the epidemic.[8] This was a bold and courageous step.

Nonetheless, some months later, she felt the urge to be on the move again. Her 'rootlessness', it seemed, took hold, and she returned to Gorgona to wind up her affairs relating to the hotel she had left behind. She found things had changed little there. At that time she also took the opportunity to visit Panama City with her brother, finding it an old-fashioned place with stone houses, almost all of which had been taken over by traders as stores. She then opened a store in Navy Bay, which she ran for the next three months. Here too she found that things were not much different. If anything, the place was even more lawless, characterised by ongoing quarrels, violence and bloodshed. There was no peace to be found. Here, again, we see Mary the opportunist, ready to take the next chance. Indeed, when an opportunity did present itself at Escribanos, one of the New Granada Gold Mining Company stations some 70 miles from Navy Bay, Mary took it. Legend had it that there were ancient treasures at various remote sites near the village. But getting there was a time-consuming business which Mary could ill afford, and even when she got there, the yield of gold, as she put it, 'did not repay the labour and capital necessary to extract it from the quartz'.[9]

Always observant and ready to learn, she was fascinated by the Alcalde (magistrate) of Escribanos, Carlo Alexander. She approved of his handling of the gold mania. The mine belonged to him, and she identified him clearly as a 'black man' who was fond of talking of his early life in slavery and how he had escaped enslavement. The superintendent of this mine was Thomas Day, whose invitation had led to Mary being in Escribanos, and who was a distant cousin of her deceased husband. Day treated her kindly, and having been the Alcalde's guest, in the twelve weeks she was there, she had grown to appreciate the new experience to the extent that for a while she was caught up with prospecting for gold. More and more, at this time, she was guided by the experience she gained. She learned fast as her powers of observation developed. Some years later, she recalled these last days of her travels in Central America. With remarkable clarity, she noted: 'The foreigners were just as troublesome in this little out-of-the-way place as they were, and are, in every other part of Central America; and quarrels were as frequent in our little community as at Cruces or Navy Bay.'[10]

Before she had left Jamaica for Escribanos, it is more than likely that she would have read the news of the 'war in the east', which related to tensions and conflict between

Russia and Turkey. By the early spring of 1854, while she was still in Kingston, British soldiers stationed there would have read and spoken about reports in *The Times* newspaper, which circulated among them. One of these accounts in *The Times* related the brutal Russian attacks which resulted in the deaths of thousands of Turks:

> The manner in which these attacks have been conducted, and the tone in which these victories have been celebrated, is sufficient proof that [Russia] will not easily desist from this war, and, though we regret none of the protracted efforts which have been made to avert so great an evil, we are not the less prepared to meet it in the last resort by a vigorous resistance.[11]

In the face of this aggression, the British and French governments, the report added, were called upon to make a prompt decision. Consequently, Britain and France joined Turkey in the Crimean War.

The British army had not fought a major European war since 1815, and the administrative problems of mobilising a large body of men were daunting. The armed forces were ill-equipped, and bureaucratic incompetence created chaotic scenes at the front, namely a lack of proper clothes, food, tents, medicines and medical attention. The camps soon became breeding grounds for disease, a problem that was compounded by mismanagement and neglect. The rising number of deaths due to disease, far in excess of

those who died in combat, aroused growing public interest in Britain. The stark accounts from the war zone by
William Howard Russell, *The Times* war correspondent,
led to a public outcry, an upsurge of public sympathy and
the creation of the Crimean Fund.[12]

Mary's upbringing, her ups and downs, her travels and
her general experience in Jamaica and Central America
were invaluable. They prepared her physically, mentally
and spiritually for future undertakings, for more ambitious travels and work that had already entered her lively
mind. If the West Indies was a far outpost of the British
Empire, developments in the Crimea promised a greater,
even more central theatre of operations, which would be
admirably suited to Mary's opportunistic designs as she
left Escribanos and embarked on her journey to England.

It may come as a surprise to some readers to learn
how eager Mary was to witness the Crimean conflict.
Her longing to see and experience war sounds naïve and
extraordinary to us today, especially because she was such
a caring person. But she wrote, 'when I was told that many
of the regiments I had known so well in Jamaica had left
England for the scene of action, the desire to join them
became stronger than ever.'[13] From then on, she was propelled forward as if by an obsession, and soon found
herself standing for long periods in deep thought as she
scanned a map of the world. Her eager eyes looked for the
Crimea. And there it was, marked by a red cross. She traced
the route from Britain to the Crimea, and her growing

preoccupation with the difficulties of getting there would vanish. As thoughts of how to get to that place on the map persisted, she had several conversations with friends, mulling it over in her mind, and found that 'the best scheme I could devise seemed so wild and improbable, that I was fain to resign my hopes for a time'.[14]

And so, some 3,000 miles away from England, she first concentrated on making the journey to England from Navy Bay before considering any further steps. Eventually the long voyage began, and in the autumn of 1854 Mary arrived in London, where she closely monitored news from the Crimea. The Battle of the Alma had already been fought. She thought of her 'old friends' who were, at the time, just outside Sebastopol. Above all else, she struggled with finding a solution to the problem of how to join them there. But as such thoughts overwhelmed her, she had the presence of mind enough to step back a little and appraise what else was passing through her mind. In London she reflected that, like others, she too had been caught up in speculation on gold mines, which seemed so feasible in New Granada at the time, but which now, viewed from her London perspective, seemed wild and improbable. This was far easier than her growing concern over an unknown battleground.

But with the passage of time, her desire had grown so much that she felt compelled to be of service. She was eager to join her 'old friends of the 97th, 48th, and other regiments, battling with worse foes than yellow fever or cholera'.[15] This last statement about the Russians was not to imply that they were to be compared with diseases and were therefore less than men. On the contrary, men were men – but thoughts of her compatriots so overwhelmed her that speculation in gold gave way to Mary devoting all her energy to her new scheme.

She was realistic about it and admitted, 'Heaven knows it was visionary enough!'[16] For one thing, she was a stranger, entirely unknown amidst the bustle of the teeming millions of the metropolis. She was overwhelmed by the experience of being in London again. Yet here, in the heart of the British Empire, her flagging spirits were bolstered. This was the most extraordinary place she had ever visited, but she had no friends who could help in her venture, and she lamented that nobody 'would understand why I desired to go, and what I desired to do when I got there'.[17] Even with careful accounting, making the near 3,000-mile trip seemed far-fetched. She could not be anything less than realistic. She worried that friends would not support her for long. There was also the problem of convincing the British public that an unknown Creole woman would be useful to their army before Sebastopol. Once again, she thought this too improbable an achievement to be thought of for an instant. She continued to wrestle with the idea and, as it was, sheer persistence and circumstances led her on. Amidst the London winter, she pondered the grim news from the war zone. Now she learned of various quarters of mismanagement, want and suffering among the

British forces in the Crimea, and, after the battles of Balaclava and Inkerman, of the fearful storm of 14 November
1854, in which large quantities of supplies were lost when
sixteen ships were sunk in Balaclava harbour. Her worst
fears were realised: it had become increasingly clear that
the need for help was urgent, that the hospitals were full to
suffocation, that scarcity and exposure were the fate of all
in the camps. Such news intensified her patriotic feelings,
compounded by further depressing reports of hundreds
who were wounded and dying at the Scutari Hospital,
where the medical facilities were woefully inadequate to
provide shelter, and the small staff was unable to cope with
the regular flow of shiploads of casualties sent to them
across the storm-tossed Black Sea.

With each day, it seemed, the news that reached London
was less and less encouraging, and by now Mary was utterly
convinced of the dire need in the Crimea. So too were the
people of England who, as Mary later reflected, set about
repairing 'past neglect'. Furthermore, she tried to capture
something of the national spirit that was engendered:

In every household busy fingers were working for the
poor soldier – money flowed in golden streams wherever need was – and Christian ladies, mindful of the
sublime example, "I was sick, and ye visited me," has-
tened to volunteer their services by those sick-beds
which only women know how to soothe and bless.[18]

Mary felt at one with England's women, but what set her apart was that she harboured a greater desire to be in 'active sympathy' with the British soldiers at war. Although she was an outsider, she was not ashamed to confess sharing in the 'general enthusiasm' which strengthened her longing to be 'where the sword or bullet had been busiest, and pestilence most rife'.[19] Her confidence was boosted by her background and experience. With hindsight, she recorded:

> I had seen much of sorrow and death elsewhere, but they had never daunted me; and if I could feel happy binding up the wounds of quarrelsome Americans and treacherous Spaniards, what delight should I not experience if I could be useful to my own "sons," suffering for a cause it was so glorious to fight and bleed for![20]

Now, all doubts about reaching the scene of action had disappeared. She was positive, focused and determined to achieve her goal. Her mind was made up that 'if the army wanted nurses, they would be glad of me, and with all the ardour of my nature, which ever carried me where inclination prompted, I decided that I would go to the Crimea'.[21] More and more, she was driven each day to do something, as the Crimea beckoned. A few years later, she reflected upon her decision, writing, 'I should have given up the scheme a score of times in as many days; so regularly did each successive day give birth to a fresh set of rebuffs and disappointments.'[22] As it was, little did she know that the Crimea and her Crimean exploits would give rise to the single most comprehensive and detailed record that we have about her.

What were the disappointments Mary wrote about? She felt she was well qualified for the work to be done, and as she mulled over the prospects, feeling that she would be the right woman in the right place, her confidence was high. It was this sense of self (and a certain degree of audacity) that moved her to present herself at the War Office to serve as a hospital nurse. She was all the more encouraged because she had already dealt with diseases such as cholera, diarrhoea and dysentery that were rife in the Crimea. In the strict professional sense, the accusation of presumption on her part would be inappropriate. She was in no doubt that her services as a nurse would be complementary to the efforts of the overworked doctors, and there were many who would testify to her knowledge and experience.

If the application she made at the War Office was an example of her tenacity, it proved to be a waste of time. Nonetheless, the appearance of this extraordinary 50-year-old un-English woman was so unusual that it caused a good deal of awkwardness among War Office officials. Years later, she wrote, 'I have reason to believe that I considerably interfered with the repose of sundry messengers, and disturbed, to an alarming degree, the official gravity of some nice gentlemanly young fellows, who were working out their salaries in an easy, offhand way.'[23] Thus she had failed in her 'ridiculous' attempt to get an interview with the Secretary of War, but, undeterred, she approached the Quartermaster-General's department. Here too she was met with much 'polite enjoyment' and amusement by the gentlemen she spoke to, who, in turn, referred her to the medical department. This too was worth a try. But alas, she grew tired of the rebuffs. The experienced nurse and doctress was clearly hurt by these consecutive disappointments. How much more could she – would she – take? Three years later, she wrote that 'not for a single instant [was she] going to blame the authorities who would not listen to the offer of a motherly yellow woman to go to the Crimea and nurse her "sons" there', since the officials in the War Office knew nothing of her experience and knowledge gained in the West Indies, despite the references she had.[24] She was, however, unhappy with the official attitude toward her, and with hindsight she expressed her reservations:

> War, I know, is a serious game, but sometimes very humble actors are of great use in it, and if the reader, when he comes in time to peruse the evidence of those who had to do with the Sebastopol drama, of my share in it, will turn back to this chapter, he will confess perhaps that, after all, the impulse which led me to the War Department was not unnatural.[25]

Each time Mary was stopped, she resorted to other plans. Now her attention was shifted to a new scheme – one which she confessed was 'worse devised than the one which had failed' – to enlist with the nurses who were to go out to the Crimea to join Florence Nightingale.[26] The desire to be with her 'sons' had not diminished one iota. If anything, it had increased. Though establishment figures may have perceived her gender to be a problem, Mary Seacole never saw it so. Being a person of colour and hailing from one of the oldest and largest former slavery-based colonies in the West Indies were barriers limiting women from the British Empire. Overall, women, including Europeans, were denied their rights. But, as Mary was gradually finding out, she had other disadvantages, even though she was well qualified for a nursing job. She wrote, 'Feeling that I was one of the very women they most wanted, experienced and fond of the work, I jumped at once to the conclusion that they would gladly enrol me in their number.'[27] But although she waited patiently to be given official consent to enlist, she had to abandon that hope after being told that the full complement of nurses had already been secured and that her offer 'could not be entertained'. This was the stock answer to candidates who were regarded as unsuitable. Thus, Mary was turned down for a nursing post. Her determination undimmed and shored up by patriotism, she decided to try once more. This time, she sought an interview with one of Nightingale's colleagues, a woman who proved to be no less obstructive. 'I read in her face the fact,' Mary wrote, 'that had there been a vacancy, I should not have been chosen to fill it.' [28]

In spite of these rejections, as a last resort, Mary turned to the managers of the Crimean Fund to see if they would assist her by paying her passage to the Crimea. She hoped that there would be work for her to do – but this attempt also failed. It was one more disappointment, but perhaps it was one too many, and it took its toll. She now had to face facts, and did so in the cold twilight of one winter's evening. Although she did not admit it at the time, the cumulative effect of these negative responses was so great that it was still strong when, years later, she reflected upon the ruins of her ambitions:

> I was so conscious of the unselfishness of the motives which induced me to leave England – so certain of service I could render among the sick soldiery, and yet I found it so difficult to convince others of these facts. Doubts and suspicions arose in my heart for the first and last time, thank Heaven. Was it possible that American prejudices against colour had some root here? Did these ladies shrink from accepting my aid because my blood flowed beneath a somewhat duskier skin than theirs?

The predicament she was in drove her to tears. The London streets were bleak and empty, the cold weather keeping the crowds away. She was grief-stricken and doubting the minds of the authorities. How could they deny her? The questions occupying her mind deepened her unhappiness so much that she began to pray aloud in public, attracting strange looks from passers-by. But however odd her behaviour might have seemed to those who saw her at the time, she felt justified in explaining it to her readers many years later, writing, 'you must all remember that I am one of an impulsive people, and find it hard to put that restraint upon my feelings which to you is so easy and natural.'[29]

After this 'natural' release of pent-up emotion arising from consecutive disappointments, Mary felt refreshed the next day. She felt relieved, ready to face all comers. She was filled with renewed hope and determination to go to the Crimea, but the problem remained: how would she go? This was the central question and, all things considered, she answered it forthrightly. The question of money was paramount, especially because she could now see no way of getting there except at her own expense. This was the bottom line. Her thoughts turned to those whom she had helped in the past, both patients and doctors. Many of them were now in the Crimea. This was the only way forward, she reasoned, writing, 'If the authorities had allowed me, I would willingly have given them my services as a nurse; but as they declined them, should I not open an hotel for invalids in the Crimea in my own way?'[30] She was now seeing the British officials very differently, and she would proceed independently of them. As she argued, after all, the authorities had hardly any more idea about her intended destination, the Crimea, than she did. So, having made up her mind, she took the next positive step. She had cards printed and sent to her friends in the Crimea, which read:

BRITISH HOTEL
Mrs Mary Seacole
(*Kingston, Jamaica*)
Respectfully announces to her former kind friends, and to the Officers of the Army and Navy generally: That she has taken her passage in the screw-steamer Hollander, to start from London on the 25th of January, intending on her arrival at Balaclava to establish a mess table and comfortable quarters for sick and convalescent officers.[31]

This was a truly bold venture, and Mary estimated her cards would arrive in the Crimea in about a week or so. The comforts of her hotel would be especially welcomed by the needy soldiers, many of whom were in poor accommodation.

As it was, luck smiled on Mary. While her new plan was maturing, she renewed her acquaintance with Thomas Day in England. It was her good fortune that he was on his way to Balaclava on shipping business. Mary laid her plans before him. He recognised her courage, enthusiasm and commitment, and, after some discussion, they agreed to open a store as well as a hotel near the camp. However fanciful it might have seemed, this was the origin of the firm Seacole and Day. But it was also the continuation of a relationship between Mary and Day that had started much earlier.[32] Important as these new arrangements were, Mary kept them separate from the main object of her voyage. With the help of a medical friend, most of her money was invested in medicines which she felt would be useful. What was left of her funds was spent on 'home comforts'.

The moment of truth arrived; the time of departure was nigh. And so Mary boarded the *Hollander*, which left England on 27 January and sailed on with hope and great expectations. Once on board the ship, Mary was gripped by a pang of sadness. Just then, she happened to meet a friend, who cheered her up as she gazed at the shores of England sinking beneath the sea. It was a bittersweet moment. Filled with private thoughts, she averted her gaze eastward as the ship plied its way towards Turkey.

4

Onward, At Last

The journey to Constantinople was, as Mary put it, 'interesting', and she boasted of being a good sailor. All the travelling she had previously done from Jamaica to Central America and to London now served her in good stead. Also in her favour was a robust constitution which helped her on the voyage, during which the weather was fine generally. It was smooth sailing as each day diminished the doubts of success in Mary's mind. It was all real and happening. She was convinced of the rightness of what she was doing. It was a positive step toward achieving her goal.

When the ship stopped briefly at Gibraltar, Mary took advantage of a few hours on shore. Ever curious, one could imagine her vigilantly seeking out the chance for a good deal. Like a latter-day shopaholic, she was bargain hunting – and she needed to be so inclined, for every moment from now on was an opportunity to stock up for her planned store. But instead of the bargains she was hoping to find at the foreign marketplace, she heard someone exclaim, 'Why, bless my soul, old fellow, if this is not our good old

Mother Seacole!'[1] The voice came from a soldier whom Mary remembered from when he had been in the 48th regiment and frequented her Kingston house. He was among the wounded men who had been invalided and sent back from the Crimea. He was determined not to let her go without some socialising. Soon Mary, the solider and his friend were talking of old times over some very nasty wine.

"And you are going to the front, old lady – you, of all people in the world?" The soldier asked.

"Why not, my sons? Won't they be glad to have me there?" Mary responded.

Seeing her determination and hearing the strength and tone of her voice, the Irish soldier answered affirmatively, "By Jove! Yes, mother."[2]

The Irishman's response was not exaggerated, but quite genuine. Women were few and far between in these places, and the wounded men were glad to have female company. They warmed to Mary's presence, as most people did. As the Irishman put it, 'It isn't many women – God bless them! – we've had to spoil us out there. But it's not the place even for you, who know what hardship is. You'll never get a roof to cover you at Balaclava, nor on the road either.' Though she needed no reminding, they talked about some of the difficulties that awaited Mary. But such talk could not shake her resolve. 'Do you think I shall be of any use to you when I get there?' Mary asked, and they replied, 'Surely.'

'Then I'll go,' she said, 'were the place a hundred times worse than you describe it.'[3] Mary knew she had to be tough and adaptable to survive the remarkable journey she had undertaken. The line her finger had followed across the world map some months earlier now looked very real. A realist, she recognised the necessity of sleeping rough, 'on straw, like Margery Daw', as she put it.[4] Three years on, she remembered fondly these soldiers, their merry laughter and their good wishes for success in her plan. They also expressed concern for their friends and colleagues whom they had left behind. Before parting company with Mary, they voiced the hope of meeting her again. Like a much-needed tonic, this interlude on shore lifted Mary's spirits appreciably.

The ship's next stop was Constantinople, where Mary's expectations were not met. She was clearly unimpressed. Put simply, she could not get on with the Turks she had met at the quayside. Amidst her trying moments, she had some respite in the form of news she had been expecting from someone. That person was Thomas Day, whose letters had arrived at the local post office. But her expectations were dashed, for she found that Day's news was not very good. His account of Balaclava and camp life was 'very dreary'. There was no reason why Mary should not believe him, and it almost convinced her that she should end her journey there. She was willing to allow intuition to play a significant part in her deliberations and decisions, but now was the time for more reflection. Then, to her relief, she read Day's instructions about the things that she should buy to advance their joint project and thus bring her closer to her objective. These crucial last words dispelled any doubts in Mary's mind. And so she set about her work, which included making the purchases that Day had recommended.

Also in her possession at this time was a letter of recommendation from a 'Dr F—' which Mary carried on her way to the Scutari Hospital to see Nightingale. What she could only have imagined back in Jamaica and during her depressing, lonely days in London gave way to the reality that now appeared before her. The dull-looking hospital and the gloom and sadness amidst the rows of sick and dying made Mary tearful. She was, however, not without hope. After a while, and being in an environment which, to some degree, she recognised from elsewhere, she was soon feeling better. Having scrutinised her surroundings, she described them thus:

> The men were, many of them, very quiet. Some of the convalescent formed themselves into little groups around one who read a newspaper; others had books in their hands, or by their side, where they had fallen when slumber overtook the readers, while hospital orderlies moved to and fro, and now and then the female nurses, in their quiet uniform, passed noiselessly on some mission of kindness.[5]

Mary's reputation had preceded her. She came into contact with another of her 'old acquaintances', who guided her through the wards. She noted how busy the nurses were as they attended to their urgent tasks. Her acquaintance was a 'Sergeant T—' from the 97th Regiment whom she had known in Jamaica. He was recovering from dysentery and was eager to get back to the heat of battle. His delight in seeing Mary again was evident. He updated her on his life story, and he took her to the sickbeds of others she had known at home. It was an odd sight, but she was pleasantly surprised by the patients' responses. The eyes of many would 'glisten', she wrote, at the sight of the familiar face of an old friend in such an unlikely place as the Turkish barracks.

'Mother Seacole! Mother Seacole!' an excitable voice resounded. In turn, Mary warmed to it and offered a few words of comfort to the wounded man who had spoken. He became more excited when she told him she was on her way to the front. As a victim of scurvy and with confidence in her capabilities, he urged Mary to take vital supplies of vegetables and eggs that were necessary to the wellbeing of the men at the front.

The awareness with which Mary approached her vocation of caring was reflected in her thoughts at this time. In spite of the risk of giving offence to the staff or patients, she was unable to ignore the obvious need for helping hands in such situations. Until now, she had offended no one with either her actions or behaviour, but she thought she might have come close to doing so on one occasion when a doctor observed her actions. At first, she wrote, he responded with 'surprise' and 'alarm' when she replaced a bandage. But when she was through, he thanked her politely.[6]

This affirmation of her skill and knowledge was timely, for not only did she get the fillip that she needed but, most importantly, it came from an English doctor. It seems likely that had it come from someone of another nationality, it may well have had less impact upon her. Her sense of her Britishness, never in doubt, was, it seemed, now most pronounced.

This experience further boosted her confidence. But although she was drawing ever closer, she was still not yet at the scene of war. Already forewarned by the 'fearful miles of suffering' at the Scutari Hospital, she wondered what it might be like closer to the front. For now, here at the hospital, the cries of pain and agony echoed about her as her soothing hands worked to bring relief. Nevertheless, Mary felt she had to move on. There was no time to waste.

It was about this time that she sought to present her letter of introduction to Nightingale. After being guided along passages and corridors that were all used as sick wards, Mary eventually reached that section of the building known as the 'corner tower', which housed the nurses. Here, she met Mrs B—, an official of some authority at the hospital, who, as Mary put it, 'felt more surprise [at my arrival] than she could politely show'.[7] Unruffled by this,

Mary handed Dr F—'s letter to the woman, who took it to Nightingale. When she returned, she asked Mary to wait until Nightingale was free to see her. While Mary waited, Mrs B—, with the same look of curiosity and surprise, took the opportunity of putting more questions to her. Underlying all was the question: what was the purpose of Mrs Seacole coming out to that desolate place? Mary's answer was frank: to be of use somewhere. Mary gives us some idea of her dogged determination to be of assistance by her declaration that she would gladly work for the wounded 'in return for bread and water'.

But Mary was saved from further thoughts of this kind when Mrs B—, thinking that Mary sought employment at Scutari Hospital, said, 'Miss Nightingale has the entire management of our hospital staff, but I do not think that any vacancy—' Before she could finish, Mary interrupted her: 'Excuse me, ma'am, but I am bound for the front in a few days.'[8] Thus this interesting episode ended, but Mary noted that when Mrs B— walked away, she looked even more surprised than ever. Mary waited for about half an hour before she was allowed to see Nightingale. Face to face, it was a meeting of historic significance, for here were two women of their time, both motivated by a common cause: to serve Britain. They were 19th-century women from opposite ends of the socio-economic spectrum: one white and from the heart of the Empire, the other a person of colour from a colonial outpost; one a pioneering paid administrator at the beginning of the new profession of nursing, the other a sutler (army camp follower) who paid her own way and roughed it towards the war zone; one young, the other much older. How did they perceive each other? In spite of their differences, this is how Mary described the Englishwoman whose reputation grew with each day:

> A slight figure in the nurses' dress; with a pale, gentle, and withal firm face, resting lightly in the palm of one white hand, while the other supports the elbow – a position which gives to her countenance a keen inquiring expression, which is rather marked. Standing thus in repose, and yet keenly observant – the greatest sign of impatience at any time a slight, perhaps unwitting motion of the firmly planted right foot – was Florence Nightingale – that Englishwoman whose name shall never die, but sound like music on the lips of British men until the hour of doom.[9]

From this description of the 'Lady with the Lamp', it seemed that even Mary was impressed by the appearance of the English nurse, whom she had heard of only very recently. But what was Nightingale's response? According to Mary, Nightingale read Dr F—'s letter, which lay on the table beside her, and in her gentle but eminently practical and business-like way she asked, 'What do you want, Mrs Seacole – anything that we can do for you? If it lies in my power, I shall be very happy.'[10] Although these words were well received, as it was there were nothing that Nightingale could do for Mary. The fact remained that no offer of employment was made to her.

Mary's next request was of greater immediacy – a bed for the night, because she had missed the boat back to her ship and thought it safer to spend the night at the Scutari Hospital. But even this request did not have the best of outcomes. Eventually a bed was found in the washerwoman's quarters. As if that were not bad enough, the night proved to be most uncomfortable, with fleas sharing Mary's bed. After breakfast the next morning, she duly made her way back to the *Hollander*.

Once there, she transferred her things from the ship that had brought her thus far to the *Albatross*. This was a trying task, for she had to overcome strong currents and hurricane winds, enduring an hour of terrible anxiety and fear, before she reached the *Albatross*'s side. After her miserable night, she now had to climb on deck drenched and wretched. Adding to her anxiety was some bad news from Day about the situation in Balaclava to which she was travelling. In these depressing circumstances, Mary was thankful that her companions on board were of a cheerful disposition, and after the hazards of crossing the Black Sea, she described her excitement when she saw the rocky coast which heralded her arrival at Balaclava. Mary was relieved by the order she found in Balaclava Harbour. She was filled with joy when Day visited her on board the *Albatross*. This was the crucial moment when, Mary said, 'our plans were

laid'. She bade farewell to the *Albatross* but, with no alter-
native lodgings until the future was decided upon in more
detail with Day, she took quarters on board the *Medora*,
another ship which had been hired by the government at
great cost as an ammunition ship. Once she came to terms
with her accommodation on the moored ship, the first
thing Mary did was to let her friends know that she had
moved to the Crimea and that their help was most welcome.
At Balaclava, her earlier discomfiture was soothed by the
pleasant surprises of re-acquainting herself with people
she had known in Jamaica. Captain Peel, commander of
the Naval Brigade, and Major-General Sir John Campbell
were among those who welcomed her. They assured her
of every assistance, which was gratefully received, all the
more because there was so much to do. She also met a man
described as 'poor H. Vicars, whose kind face had so often
lighted up my old house in Kingston'.[11] He took Mary by
the hand, and she felt odd and grateful for his reassuring
personality and presence 'in this out-of-the-way corner of
the world'. Her confidence boosted, she declared, 'I never
felt so sure of the success of any step as I did of this, before I
had been a week in Balaclava.' Nonetheless, she had plenty
of difficulties on a range of matters in this foreign land.[12]
Having braved and survived the unpredictable sea, Mary
found that her feet were once more firmly planted on dry
land. The planning stages of her bold, imaginative Crimean
enterprise had led to a new place and thus to the practicali-
ties of the venture. By now she felt better prepared. During

the six weeks of her stay in Balaclava, she spent her days on shore and her nights on board ship. It was a most unsettling, uncomfortable time, but there was no deviation from her objective. As her ideas crystallised, she recognised that a systematic approach was the only way forward. Each day, she apportioned time to receiving visitors and selling stores, but she never lost sight of the pressing humanitarian work of caring for the sick and dying. This she regarded as her chief occupation, on which there could be no compromise. Commenting on this, she wrote:

> I never allowed any business to interfere [with] helping the doctors to transfer the sick and wounded from the mules and ambulances into the transports that had to carry them to the hospitals of Scutari and Buyukdere. I did not forget the main object of my journey, to which I would have devoted myself exclusively had I been allowed; and very familiar did I become before long with the sick wharf of Balaclava.

On the first day that Mary approached this 'sick wharf', a party of the sick and wounded had just arrived. Now began the essential work for which she had come. Mary heard an artilleryman groaning and went to attend to him. He had been hit on the head. Mary 'raised some tea to his baked lips [...] Then his hand touched mine, and rested there, and I heard him mutter indistinctly, as though the discovery had arrested his wandering senses – "Ha! This is surely a woman's hand.'" In response she spoke comforting words, then the wounded man whispered, 'God bless you, woman – whoever you are, God bless you!'[13] Once more, Mary describes the effect of her presence upon others. She was there to help, but did she look the part of a nurse? Who could say? At the time, nursing was in its infancy, just beginning to feel its way into becoming the vital profession it is now. Caring and saving lives were Mary's primary concerns in her early years in Jamaica and Central America, and were perhaps even more so now. Far from being a sprightly young nursing recruit, she was the opposite, popularly known as 'Mother Seacole'.

Apart from helping others, there was a side to Mary that hinted at self-satisfaction, with her stout, round appearance, of which she was proud. If Mary was conspicuous by her physical presence, clearly, in a variety of ways, she was also the most colourful person around. 'I do not think that the surgeons noticed me at first,' she explained, 'although, as this was my introduction to Balaclava, I had not neglected my personal appearance, and wore my favourite yellow dress, and blue bonnet, with the red ribbons.'[14] It was not as though she were going to a picnic. The reason, perhaps, for wearing such feminine attire in such gaudy colours was its effect on the places she visited. She hoped it would lift the spirits of many around her who were clearly in need of a boost. Fortunately for them, Mary was not simply playing a part; it was in her character to be optimistic. All those who had met her knew and felt this to be true, plus she was highly visible and unforgettable to those who had met her and benefitted from her ministrations. To see her for a second time, and more frequently, especially amidst the heart-rending bloody scenes of the war zone, was a bonus.

Critics may well lambast her for overplaying her testimonials. But in her autobiography she places eyewitness accounts before the reader, instead of proclaiming her own interpretation of her actions. Among those who would later speak about her good deeds was a captain, who became Major R— in charge of the wharf, from whom she had received a kind letter while at Balaclava. It read:

> Dear Mrs Seacole, – I am very sorry to hear that you have been unfortunate in business; but I am glad to hear that you have found friends in Lord R— and others, who are ready to help you. No one knows better than I do how much you did to help poor sick and wounded soldiers; and I feel sure you will find in your day of trouble that they have not forgotten it.[15]

This was a promising start for Mary, who regarded Major R—'s competence and sensitive approach towards the wounded very highly. Brave and experienced as Major R— was, the tragedies he witnessed on the sick wharf often unmanned him, she said. He worried a great deal about those in his charge. For Mary and the soldiers generally, such humanitarian concern was widespread. Nonetheless, she duly recognised the value of the care provided by the women who served, a contribution which, she wrote, few (if any) men could match.

In respect of the need in the Crimea, the claims she made in the West Indies, Central America and London about the importance of her role in particular, but also of women generally, were correct. In retrospect she wrote, 'Only women could have done more than they did who attended to this melancholy duty; and they, not because their hearts could be softer, but because their hands are moulded for this work.' [16] So now, amidst the smell of death, she did her best to help, even to effect some levity. She wrote that there were some cheerful scenes at the sick wharf. In fact, the courage and magnanimity of spirit among the men was astonishing to her. She said they delighted in seeing her again so far from her native Jamaica, the idyllic tropical setting of their first meeting.

Hearing the sound of her name, Mary instantly recognised a sailor from her Kingston days. 'Why, as I live, if this ain't Aunty Seacole, of Jamaica! Shiver all that's left of my poor timbers.' The tone was reminiscent of the Irishman she had met when she stepped ashore in Gibraltar. On closer inspection, she realised the man's left leg was gone, yet he kept his spirits up, saying, 'if this ain't a rum go, mates!' Over her years of mixing with the English, Mary's use of English phrases and expressions had evolved to a point where she felt they were natural and fitting as she dealt with her 'sons'.

'Ah!' she replied. 'My man, I'm sorry to see you in this sad plight.'

'Never fear for me, Aunty Seacole; I'll make the best of the leg the Rooshians have left me. I'll get at them soon again, never fear. You don't think, messmates [...] that they'll think less of us at home for coming back with a limb or so short?'

'You bear your troubles well, my son,' Mary responded.

'Eh! do I, Aunty?' he said, with a look of surprise. 'Why, look'ye, when I've seen so many pretty fellows knocked off the ship's roll altogether, don't you think I ought to be thankful if I can answer the bo'swain's call anyhow?'[17]

Such courage as this man had shown affected the men, as Mary related. 'This brave fellow,' she said, 'after he had sipped some lemonade, and laid down, when he heard the men groaning, raised his head and comforted them in the same strain again; and, it may seem strange, but it quieted them.'[18] To comfort the sick and wounded in their last days and moments, Mary made and served them sponge cakes and lemonade. Rising magnificently to the part and the occasion, like a mother, she watched over them and noted, 'They all liked the cake, poor fellows, better than anything else: perhaps because it tasted of "home".'[19] It was like home for Mary too, for now she was doing what she wholeheartedly did best: providing her special brand of care and concern always for those in need.

For some time yet, Mary lived aboard the ship, the *Medora*, to which she had been transferred. Whatever she may have imagined about life in Balaclava, it did not now surprise her. She had anticipated that life here would be rough. This was certainly the case for quite a while. The days were 'enough to try any woman's strength', and at night she was 'not always certain of repose'.[20] For a woman, and one of her size and age (she was now about 50 years old), clambering up the sides of the ship each day was not easy. Why was it so difficult just to get on deck? The staves in the ladder, Mary explained, did not reach high enough, and if they were broader it would have helped. Rarely did she complain, but this was not all that concerned her. Once aboard, there were other terrifying dangers. The *Medora* was an ammunition ship, packed with barrels of explosives – gunpowder and tons of cartridges – over which Mary and the ship's company slept. Given the volatile circumstances that justified its presence in that crowded harbour, the chances of this explosive cargo igniting were great.

Apart from sleepless nights, Mary was faced with the daytime worry of offloading her stores with the help of Greek and Maltese boatmen, most of whom she suspected of being professional thieves. If this was harassing work, even more so was the problem of protecting her property. For one thing, she could not conduct the surveillance of her property herself, for here on the wharf, she not only sold 'stores' but also administered medicines to those in need among the Land Transport and Army Works personnel. Thus, in spite of her best efforts, Mary was plagued by ubiquitous thieves, who prowled around especially at night. Their ingenuity was incredible – even worthy of admiration from Mary. 'The thievery in this little out-of-the-way port was something marvellous,' she reflected, 'and the skill and ingenuity of the operators would have reflected credit upon the *élite* of their profession practising in the most civilized city of Europe.' [21] Pragmatic and streetwise as Mary was, and as an observer of the customs and practice of different lands, she found that thievery in this part of the world was widespread and on a different scale. The thieves' targets included the likes of Mary and the English, the Turks and one another. Mary was careful to distinguish between the Turks and others, though, for they, as victims, received special treatment.

She viewed the situation as being in a state of 'predatory warfare', in which the French Zouaves were especially successful. She did not hide her admiration for these brilliant 'little fellows', a 'restless' bunch, who, when denied access to the Russians, sought action in Balaclava. Their main interest was, according to Mary, to seek 'opportunities of waging war against society at large'.[22] Although they were indiscriminate in their thievery, with no regard for the property rights of others, Mary found it all quite amusing. Indeed, two years later, she wrote about the thieves' artfulness, which won her admiration:

To see a Zouave gravely cheat a Turk, or trip up a Greek street-merchant, or Maltese fruit-seller, and scud away with the spoil, clearly stowed in his roomy red pantaloons, was an operation, for its coolness, expedition, and perfectness, well worth seeing. And, to a great extent, they escaped scatheless, for the English Provost marshal's department was rather chary of interfering with the eccentricities of our gallant allies.[23]

With each day, Mary's sympathy for the Turks grew. She thought it lamentable how they were robbed, abused and bullied and wondered why they did not show the fighting spirit of their compatriots by confronting their attackers. 'A little pluck' and 'ever so little spirit' were all they needed. But they would rather complain noisily and profusely instead of dealing with those who bullied them. It was rare that the tables were turned, and Mary only saw it happen once while she was there. She was still some distance away from the battlefront, but it was clear to Mary that Balaclava was a dangerous place:

> Had it not been for the unremitting activity of the authorities, no life would have been safe in Balaclava, with its population of villains of every nation. As it was, murder was sometimes added to robbery, and many of the rascals themselves died suspicious deaths, with the particulars of which the authorities did not trouble themselves.[24]

In spite of it all, Mary recognised the efforts that went into maintaining law and order. Her experience at Balaclava taught her tough lessons, which served her in good stead for what was to come. Finally, after leaving Balaclava, Mary arrived at the spot where she desired to be, the place where the necessary preparations in establishing her store were made.[25] Her long-held dream of reaching the front in the Crimea was now reality.

5

Prelude to War

Before proceeding with Mary Seacole's story, let us consider the context of the Crimean War and the other women who were caught up in it. By 1853, the decline of the Ottoman Empire had become a matter of concern to the great powers of Europe. The ruler of Russia, Tsar Nicholas I, referring to the Ottomans, is alleged to have informed the British Ambassador, 'We have a sick man on our hands, a man gravely ill, it will be a great misfortune if one of these days he slips through our hands, especially before the necessary arrangements are made.'[1] Each of the major powers in Europe interpreted these 'necessary arrangements' in their own way. The tsar, for example, was interested in control of Constantinople, which he saw as giving his fleet access to the warmer waters of the Mediterranean through the Bosphorus. Britain and France, already described as the 'policemen of Europe', were also interested in territorial matters. Britain viewed Russian expansion in Asia and the Middle East as a threat to its interests in the Mediterranean and in India. And while France was

keen to uphold its military prestige and further its imperial designs, Prince Albert reflected popular feeling when
he said, 'The emperor of Russia is a tyrant and the enemy
of all liberty on the Continent.'[2]

In the meantime, while the Ottoman Empire continued to decay, Russia and France, eager to extend their
imperial interests, concentrated on the ongoing dispute
concerning the rights of Christians to worship in Otto-
man-ruled Jerusalem. Before 1850, Muslim policemen
stood guard both inside and outside the Church of the
Holy Sepulchre in Jerusalem, the Church of the Nativ-
ity in Bethlehem and the Tomb of the Virgin of Geth-
semane in the hope of keeping peace between Catholics
and Greek Orthodox Christians. This dispute was not as
easy to resolve as it seemed, and in time it was used as
a pretext for a much wider struggle. Historically, France
regarded itself as the defender of Catholicism, priests and
Christian places of worship. The Ottoman Empire's weak-
ness helped matters little, because both the French and
Russian rulers felt they stood a real chance of winning
the quarrel. A victory would settle the dispute. The sub-
sequent 'war of words' drew all of Europe's great powers
into diplomatic exchanges. In the ensuing negotiations,
the three autocratic players, Tsar Nicholas I, Sultan Abdul
Mejid I and Napoleon III, failed to agree. A short time
later, the tsar forced the issue by demanding the right to
act on behalf of the millions of Orthodox Christians who
were subjects of the Ottoman Empire. This left little room

for manoeuvre, and the tsar's ultimatum was turned down by the sultan.

Russia responded in July 1853 by moving into the Ottoman principalities of Moldova and Wallachia, and on 5 October 1853 the Turks felt obliged to declare war against Russia. The Turkish Commander Omar Pasha served notice to Russia's General Mikhail Dmitrievich Gorchakov to leave the principalities in two weeks. The Russians refused to comply, and the Turks advanced on the Russians. The Turks won this confrontation. Nonetheless, the conflict persisted, and the build-up of tension resulted in another confrontation, this time at sea. Both the Turkish and Russian fleets faced each other in the Black Sea, and in November 1853 the Russian fleet destroyed a Turkish squadron in the harbour at Sinope, their use of explosive shells ushering in a new age of naval warfare and contributing to the end of wooden warships.

The Turkish defeat was on such a scale that in London it was reported as a massacre. Home Secretary Lord Palmerston's response was that 'something must be done to wipe away the stain'.[3] Thereafter, the Russian fleet sailed for Sebastopol and the British Admiralty began to consider attacking it. In Britain and France feelings ran high, and rumours of war against Russia reached fever pitch. It was thought by many young men that, should an attack take place, it would be a brief campaign and those who fought would be back home before Christmas. One of these young men was Private Timothy Gowing, a fusilier from Norwich:

[...] the Turks were trying to defend themselves against their ancient foes the Russians, and thrilling accounts were appearing in our newspapers about the different fights at the seat of war on the Danube. I was now just approaching my twentieth year [...] and the accounts that were constantly coming home from the East worked me up to try my luck, as others had done before me.[4]

And so, just 40 years after Wellington had defeated Napoleon at Waterloo, France and Britain signed a military alliance. Finally, on 28 March 1854, they entered the war.

Once war was declared, much attention shifted to the ordinary British soldier. If hitherto 'the profession of arms was still a worthy one for those who could purchase commissions, the soldier was [still] a social outcast,' a despised being, and the army was seen by its critics as a 'needless expense', a 'drag on the national economy.'[5] Indeed, the private soldier found it useless to protest against the stigma of his lowly status. But now, with the looming war, the 'popular mood underwent one of its many surprising changes. The despised redcoat was seen in a new light as war fever reached the level of hysteria [...] cheer boys, cheer'.[6] The British troops were the best-dressed expeditionary force ever: the Hussars, Light Dragoons, Heavy Dragoons and Lancers looked splendid. But it was argued that their regalia served no practical purpose. Moreover, the 'Army of the East' was hopelessly ill equipped.

As the contingents marched out of their barracks on their way to the front, another surprising feature of the Crimean War was revealed: that behind each regiment came a company of women. They were described as 'ill-assorted', some as 'slatterns', some with 'pinched' looks, some dressed in odd clothing, but most were 'wrapped in shawls'. Overall, they were a motley crew, among whom were 'gaunt and haggard faces; raw boned scrawny types that were almost devoid of sex; faces inured to hardship yet still in a mould of self-respect'.[7] As the men marched away, these hardened women followed. They tried to keep pace with the column, but some fell behind, while others were forced to trot. Determined, 'each woman carried a bundle which held all her possessions'.[8] As it was, they were bound for a future where conditions, it was thought, could hardly be worse than those they were leaving behind – for they too were off to the 'Seat of War'. They were the army wives and regimental women.

There were clear indications that the army discouraged marriage among its non-commissioned ranks. The stone-barracks habitation of soldiers was no place for women and children. Commanding officers saw women as 'encumbrances' who detracted from the essentially displaced life of a soldier. Nonetheless, the presence of women could not be ruled out, 'even though little provision was made to settle them in quarters'.[9] By all accounts, life in the barracks was appalling. According to historian Piers Compton:

The atmosphere of the large unventilated rooms, kept airless for the sake of warmth[,] was frequently poisoned by badly positioned drains. The death rate from tuberculosis among soldiers [...] was five times as great as among civilians. These were the conditions in which married soldiers and their wives set up their homes, separated one from another by flimsy curtains or, if they were lucky, in a corner where screens might deaden the sights, but not the sounds or smells of a never-empty barrack room. The fact that there was little prospect of improvement made these surroundings all the more depressing.[10]

To compound the problems of the soldier and his wife, consider the pay of one shilling which a private received each week. From this, 6d a week was deducted 'for rations, replacements and a never ending list of extras', which meant a severe reduction of a couple's budget. It was here, as one historian put it, that the soldier's wife came in useful: in return for their higgledy-piggledy space in barracks, the wives were granted the 'privilege' of working as washerwomen for the troops. Other wives chose to be, or were employed as, cooks or seamstresses. Some were picked to be nursemaids to officers' families and were regarded as a 'better' type of regimental woman. Generally, though, most of these women worked in the barracks' laundries. With time, they became so toughened that they gained a reputation for being 'rough and ready' travellers. Yet it was found, and surprisingly so, 'that some barrack women retained their innate sterling qualities of proper pride, loyalty and devotion so that they were fully conversant with the spirit of the Regiment to which they belonged'. Nonetheless, their numbers were limited, for, according to the Queen's Regulations, an average of six wives was permitted for each company of 100 infantrymen. Many wives were so determined to join their husbands that they pleaded with officers' wives to employ them as 'maids'.[11]

And so, for better or worse, many women followed their men to the Crimean War. Early in 1854, we can picture the following scene. The Coldstream Guards' departure from St George's Barracks in London was an emotional one, which greatly affected the crowds that had gathered on the steps of St Martin-in-the-Fields and filled Trafalgar Square. Among the column of men that marched by were an estimated 32 women. The barracks vacated by the Coldstreams were, in turn, occupied by the Grenadier Guards from the Tower of London, who were expected to leave the next day at noon. The excitement among them was such that it was said none of them slept that night. Compton has described what happened next:

Tattoo sounded but no one interfered though the barrack room was filled with the men and their women-folk. At 3am the bugle sounded the roll call and companies fell in under the dim yellow light of a lantern. Two hours later, the leading files emerged through the West door of the National Gallery and once again the thoroughfares from Charing Cross and Waterloo Bridge rocketed into life.[12]

Amidst renditions of 'Rule Britannia' and 'God Save the Queen', there were patriotic shouts of 'Grenadiers remember England' as the Grenadiers marched towards Whitehall. Then people sang along as 'Annie Laurie' was played, and a 'little muster' of about twenty regimental wives did their best to keep pace with the troops as they marched past Buckingham Palace. One reporter, who took a keen interest in these women, wrote: 'The married women who [accompanied] the soldiers [can] easily be distinguished from their less fortunate companions by being laden like pack horses.' That same month, a few hundred miles away at Plymouth Quay, a more fortunate couple, Captain Henry Duberly and Fanny Duberly, embarked on the *Shooting Star*. In their wake, one nagging question remained: were the women of the army 'more to be pitied' than the regimental wives who chose to remain in England? Compton informs us of the desperation among army wives who were left behind, for whom there was 'no allowance nor provision whatever'. In the absence of their husbands, and without the means of any income, they were 'unable to keep up a regular home even if they had one, and often with children to support, their survival becomes a mystery'. Thus many wives had no option but either to turn to the local workhouse or starve.[13] But while many excluded army wives faced a bleak future at home, those thought to have been more fortunate by being in the transport ships had to endure agonies of discomfort before they experienced the hellish conditions of camp life on and near the battlefields of the Crimea.

Against this background of British women from the heart of the Empire making their way to the war zone, Mary was conspicuous not only for her colourful dress, skill and age but also because she was a woman of colour from a far-flung colonial outpost. But now here she was, among the British women, having arrived at the place where she would begin the process of building her British Hotel.

6

The British Hotel

The moment for making the British Hotel a reality had arrived. Of course, Mary could not have known at the time that this would be the beginning of a project that was to become a monument to her presence and multi-faceted work in the Crimea. Starting from scratch in this new environment, Mary set about the task of erecting the hotel, and found that its location, Spring Hill, had its own pitfalls. Finding her bearings was essential. How did she get around? She informs us that she did so sometimes on horseback, sometimes getting a lift on the commissariat carts and ammunition railway wagons. She visited Spring Hill every day and, out of necessity, had a shed erected to accommodate her. Soon she began to realise the enormity of what she had got herself into. In the circumstances, the difficulties that constructing the Seacole and Day hotel presented were clearly immense. For one thing, acquiring building materials was a major problem – 'next to impossible', she wrote. She resorted to collecting what she could find, including bits and pieces of driftwood and timber from the harbour. She then faced the task of hiring workmen. Eventually she was able to assemble a group of workers among whom were two English sailors, nick-named 'Big and Little Chips', and some Turks.

While gathering her workforce, she had made the acquaintance of the pacha who commanded the Turkish division encamped near Spring Hill. With materials and men gathered together, building work commenced, but the process proved to be far from easy or smooth. Unforeseen circumstances tested her often. On one occasion, heavy rains burst a dam, creating a deluge that swept along Spring Hill with disastrous results. Mary's 'temporary hut' was flooded, and stores of up to £200 in value were destroyed. Because Mary was unwilling to part with her belongings, the torrent that hit Spring Hill could have been tragic for her. Later she recalled: 'seeing a little box which contained some things, valuable as relics of the past, being carried away, I plunged in after it, and losing my balance, was rolled over and over by the stream, and with some difficulty reached the shore'.[1] Without questioning her fearlessness and impulsiveness, could this passage be a retrospective exaggeration? The next day, the building site looked a sad wreck, winning the sympathy and help of British commander Lord Raglan's men, who were passing by.

In time, Mary realised the importance of establishing local contacts, and soon her friendship with the pacha grew stronger. Indeed, their relationship was so warm that some in Spring Hill felt the pacha was showing unusual interest in her. But he had three wives, and Mary felt he had no need for another one. The pacha's greatest desire was to be familiar with the English language, and to this end he turned to Mary for guidance and help. He 'would try hard to sow a few English sentences in his treacherous memory,' she wrote, but his progress was slow.[2] He tried hard, but could only manage about half a dozen sentences, and Mary was convinced that, had they continued their pupil–teacher relationship further, there would have been no significant progress in spite of the pacha's best efforts. But although he was clearly not destined for linguistic excellence, the pacha maintained warm and friendly relations with Mary, and often his band provided music at Spring Hill. Such interludes soothed the jangled nerves of Mary's customers, which she appreciated. In time, she came to regard this Turkish gentleman as a capital neighbour whose rank and orders afforded her the protection she so clearly needed. Yet the thieves were never far away. Naturally, she was sad when the pacha and his men departed for Kamara. The loss of her Turkish neighbours was a blow felt in more ways than one. For quite a while, Mary felt exposed on Spring Hill. It was only when men of the Land Transport Corps encamped near Mary's land that she felt reasonably safe. She wished she could see more of her business partner, Thomas Day, who, she said, 'rarely returned to Spring Hill until nightfall', meaning that his responsibilities were left unfulfilled.[3] Nonetheless, Mary did the best she could to make progress. The necessary assistance she received came from those she had recruited. She got by on her 'reputation for determination and courage – a poor delusion, which I took care to heighten by the judicious display of a double-barrelled pistol, lent me for the purpose by Mr Day, and which I couldn't have loaded to save my life.'[4]

So, Mary had to be vigilant as she supervised the building of the British Hotel. As the end of the summer months approached, the project was almost complete. But, even months later, Mary reflected that the hotel 'never was completed, and when we left the Hill, a year later, it still wanted shutters.'[5] Yet it was regarded by all as the most complete thing there. At a cost of some £800, the British Hotel and its surrounding buildings covered about an acre of land. It was as perfect as they could make it, Mary insisted. She described the hotel and storehouse thus:

> [...] a long iron room, with counters, closets and shelves; above it was another room, used by us for storing our goods, and above this floated a large union-jack. Attached to this building was a little kitchen, not unlike a ship's caboose – all stoves and shelves. In addition to the iron house were two wooden houses, with sleeping apartments for myself and Mr Day, out-houses for our servants, a canteen for the soldiery, and a large enclosed yard for our stock, full of stables, low huts, and sties. Everything, although rough and unpolished,

was comfortable and warm; and there was a complete-
ness about the whole which won general admiration.[6]

Gazing at the hotel, what satisfaction must Mary have
felt. She was the woman who foresaw this need. She was
the right woman, in the right place, at the right time.
Despite mismanagement and problems in the camp, she
now had a clearer view of why she was there. Within her
own sphere of influence, she was determined to bring
comfort and order to Spring Hill. In the days that passed,
those who visited the hotel were refreshed. Encouraged,
Mary was careful to spare no expense in stocking her store
with provisions from an anchor down to a needle. The
most pressing problem, as previously, was that of thieves,
who kept an eye out for anything and everything they
felt could be lifted. While she braved the cold and rainy
Crimean weather, it was the thieves who posed her the
greatest threat. Mary felt besieged by human thieves and
animal ones – the rats. She tried to combat them, but the
extent of thievery was overwhelming and cost her dearly:

Although we kept a sharp lookout by day, and paid a
man five shillings a night as watchman, our losses were
very great. During the time we were in the Crimea we
lost over a score of horses, four mules, eighty goats, many
sheep, pigs, and poultry, by thieving alone. We missed
in a single night forty goats and seven sheep, and on
Mr Day's going to headquarters with intelligence of the

disaster, they told him that Lord Raglan had recently received forty sheep from Asia, all of which had disappeared in the same manner. The geese, turkeys and fowls vanished by scores.[7]

Mary worried about her livestock and food stores, but she also needed to ensure her personal safety. And with good reason: she wrote about her fears at Spring Hill after the brutal murder of her washerwoman and all her seven children. The whole camp was stunned, and Mary's fears increased because the murderer, or murderers, were still at large. Mary's losses from theft were, at times, serious. Among the items taken from her stock were tablecloths, domestic linen and most of her clothes. Fortunately, she was able to buy more.[8] Nonetheless, Mary, the opportunistic multi-talented businesswoman, proceeded to engage in what she had come out to the Crimea to do.

Following the opening of the Seacole and Day establishment, as winter approached, even though roaring winds and rain played havoc and made roads impassable, officers found their way to the hotel. Shortages were glaringly obvious, namely the want of shirts and socks, pocket handkerchiefs and wrapping paper. Mary also realised that the acquisition of a number of things were necessary for her to truly deliver the home comforts which she promised the soldiers who congregated at Spring Hill (which became synonymous with the British Hotel). Hungry officers made their way along muddy roads to see what Mother

Seacole had in store. Her cooking, either for lunch or dinner, was eagerly anticipated by many who had become regulars. Meat, pies, rice pudding, pastry and rhubarb tarts were among the things she served up for her 'sons'. She wrote, 'I declare I never heard or read of an army so partial to pastry as that British Army before Sebastopol.'[9]

Indeed, it was not unusual to see a crowd of officers in high spirits in the kitchen of Mary's hotel. Sometimes, when their behaviour had tested Mary sorely, she was known to brandish an iron spoon in frustration. At such times, she wrote, 'the good-for-nothing black cooks, instead of lending me their aid, would stand by and laugh with all their teeth'.[10] Mary's establishment became a popular meeting place, a haven of rest and pleasure. In the hot weather, many flocked to the hotel just for Mary's specials: claret and cider cups, and other cooling drinks. Mary spoke a good deal about mothering the men, ensuring that they had adequate and well-prepared food. When she related how funny some things were, she did not neglect to represent the tragic side also.

As she began to find her feet, so to speak, in that new and dangerous environment, what must it have been like? In her autobiography, she begged the reader's permission before describing one day of her life in the Crimea:

I was generally up and busy by daybreak, sometimes earlier, for in the summer my bed had no attractions strong enough to bind me to it after four. There was plenty to do before the work of the day began. There was the poultry to pluck and prepare for cooking, which had been killed on the previous night; the joints to be cut up and got ready for the same purpose; the medicines to be mixed; the store to be swept and cleaned. Of very great importance, with all these things to see after, were the few hours of quiet before the road became alive with travellers. By seven o'clock the morning coffee would be ready, hot and refreshing, and eagerly sought for by the officers of the Army Works Corps [...] There was always a great demand for coffee by those who knew its refreshing and strengthening qualities, milk I could not give them (I kept it in tins for special use); but they had it hot and strong, with plenty of sugar and a slice of butter, which I recommend as a capital substitute for milk. From that time until nine, officers on duty in the neighbourhood, or passing by, would look in for breakfast, and about half past nine my sick patients began to show themselves. In the following hour they came thickly, and sometimes it was past twelve before I had got through this duty. They came with every variety of suffering and disease; the cases I most disliked were the frostbitten fingers and feet in the winter. That over, there was the hospital to visit across the way, which was sometimes overcrowded with patients [...] I used not always to stand upon too much ceremony when I heard of sick or wounded officers in the front. Sometimes their friends would ask me to go to them, though very often I waited for no hint, but took the chance of meeting with a kind reception. I used to think of their relatives at home, who would have given so much to possess my privilege; and more than one officer have I startled by appearing before him, and telling him abruptly that he must have a mother, wife, or sister at home whom he missed, and that he must therefore be glad of some woman to take their place.

Until evening the store would be filled with customers wanting stores, dinners, and luncheons; loungers and idlers seeking conversation and amusement; and at eight o'clock the curtain descended on that day's labour, and I could sit down and eat at leisure. It was no easy thing to clear the store, canteen, and yards; but we determined upon adhering to the rule that nothing should be sold after that hour, and succeeded. Any one who came after that time, came simply as a friend. There could be no necessity for any one, except on extraordinary occasions, when the rule could be relaxed, to purchase things after eight o'clock. And drunkenness or excess were discouraged at Spring Hill in every way; indeed, my few unpleasant scenes arose chiefly from my refusing to sell liquor where I saw it was wanted to be abused. I could appeal with a clear conscience to all who knew me there, to back my assertion that I neither permitted drunkenness among the men nor gambling among the officers. Whatever happened elsewhere, intoxication, cards, and dice were never to be seen within the precincts of the British Hotel. [...]

At first we kept our store open on Sunday from sheer necessity, but after a little while, when stores in abundance were established at Kadikoi and elsewhere, and the absolute necessity no longer existed, Sunday became a day of most grateful rest at Spring Hill. This step also met with opposition from the men; but again we were determined, and again we triumphed. I am sure we needed rest [...] although I never had a week's illness during my campaign, the labour, anxiety, and perhaps the few trials that followed it, have told upon me. I have never felt since that time the strong and hearty woman that I was when I braved with impunity the pestilence of Navy Bay and Cruces. It would kill me easily now.[11]

7

Amidst the Carnage

In her autobiography, Mary Seacole wrote that she feared seeming self-congratulatory in giving an account of her work in the Crimea, although her achievement in reaching the front at all against overwhelming odds makes some self-congratulation seem justified. 'I enter upon the particulars of this chapter with great reluctance,' she admitted, 'but I cannot omit them, for the simple reason that they strengthen my one and only claim to interest the public, viz., my services to the brave British Army in the Crimea.'[1] However, the fact that there was no shortage of other people to bear testimony to her work made it unnecessary for her to blow her own trumpet. Thus she wrote, 'I can put on record the written opinions of those who had ample means of judging and ascertaining how I fulfilled the great object which I had in view in leaving England for the Crimea.'[2]

But before doing so she felt it was important to solicit her readers' attention to her position in the camp as doctress, nurse and 'mother'. In the world of the mid-19th century, with war and sickness so widespread, Mary had always found her experience and practice of medical art useful wherever she went. Even in London, she had found her knowledge and skills to be of service to others. This was an area of nursing in which she was fully competent and confident of her abilities. But she can hardly have imagined the conditions she found in the war zone. The Crimea was a strange place, a surreal scene of overwhelming death and destruction. Mary wrote that the 'doctors were so overworked, and sickness was so prevalent, I could not be long idle; for I never forgot that my intention in seeking the army was to help the kindhearted doctors, to be useful to whom I have ever looked upon and still regard as so high a privilege'.[3]

If she felt ennobled in the doctors' company, amidst the carnage and confusion, soon Mary was surrounded by patients of her own, aiding the regimental doctors whose surplus patients found their way to the British Hotel daily for treatment and nourishing food. With no competing establishment, she made herself known and useful to an ever-growing clientele. Her easy and welcoming manner cheered the officers and men, who saw her as warm and caring, and they were reassured not only by her strong and stout motherly frame but also by the fact that she was a 'doctress and nurse'. If they did not know it at first, as each day passed the soldiers realised that she never tired in her concern for them. Mary welcomed them to partake of her home comforts instead of remaining in their cheerless huts. Writing with hindsight, she painted a picture of gloom and stark realism for readers of her autobiography. She asked them to imagine 'lying, with parched lips and fading appetite, thousands of miles from mother, wife, or sister, loathing the rough food by your side, and thinking regretfully of that English home where nothing that could minister to your great need would be left untried'.[4] Ever on the move, often on horseback, she went beyond the call of duty to please the British officers and men. She fed them, bandaged their wounds and applied her healing art; she applied soothing hands, with whispered words to comfort them. Predictably, Mary's humanitarian concern took its toll on her. Over the days and months of witnessing and feeling deep pain, her face became more careworn, the lines on her forehead more pronounced. But advancing age was no deterrent. She was ubiquitous, spreading her much-appreciated cheerfulness and her smile like rays of sunlight through the cloud of gloom and depression that hung over the area. She was now perhaps the best known of all those in Spring Hill and its ravaged environs. In such circumstances, she wrote, 'don't you think that you would welcome the familiar figure of the stout lady whose bony horse has just pulled up at the door of your hut, and whose panniers contain some cooling drink, a little broth, some homely cake, or a dish of jelly or blanc-mange'?[5] The famous British magazine *Punch* agreed with Mary Seacole and famously remarked:

That berry-brown face, with a kind heart's trace
Impressed on each wrinkle sly
Was a sight to behold, though the snow-clouds rolled
Across the iron sky.[6]

So Mary Seacole's bright personality lit up the place, giving a welcoming, homely feel in this war-torn outpost. She wrote:

I have seen many a bold fellow's eyes moisten [...] when a woman's voice and a woman's care have brought to their minds recollections of those happy English homes which some of them never saw again; but many did, who will remember their woman-comrade upon the bleak and barren heights before Sebastopol.[7]

She drew great satisfaction when she remembered them calling her 'mother'. In turn, these patriots were her 'sons', who were susceptible to things that triggered memories of home. Among her patients in the Crimea was one whom she had known in Jamaica, a winner of the Victoria Cross, who was cured by her caring hands. Later, in her autobiography, she reproduced letters from another patient who had suffered from jaundice, to whom she recommended medicine which improved his condition:

My Dear Mrs Seacole,
I have finished the bottle, which has done my

jaundice a deal of good. Will you kindly send another
by bearer.
Truly yours,
F. M.[8]

Mary added, 'It was a capital prescription which had done
his jaundice good. There was so great a demand for it, that
I kept it mixed in a large pan, ready to ladle it out to the
scores of applicants who came for it.'[9] She said her heart
bled for the suffering men to whom she played hostess at
the British Hotel.

Thus far, Mary had given her readers a good idea of her
life in the Crimea, but, writing several months later, she
offered three excuses for any historical inexactness: first,
that her memory was unreliable and she had no written
record; second, that although the reader would have had
enough of journals and chronicles of Crimean life, she
was unique in being the only historian of Spring Hill; and
third, unless she was allowed to tell her story in her own
way, she could not tell it at all.

We already know what her life was like at the British
Hotel, but what was it like out of doors, on the field of
battle? She bore witness to great events and was humbled
as they unfolded. But in her record of what she saw, inevita-
bly, there were gaps, because she could not be everywhere.
Mary attributed her absence from the scene of memorable
action to her attendance to the stricken and wounded, and
because she was either 'mixing medicines or making good

things in the kitchen of the British Hotel'.[10] Although she was in the Crimea and knew a great deal about the Battle of the Tchernaya, she did not see it from the vantage point of a hilltop. Even regarding this experience, she was aware of the discrepancy between being on the spot or near the scene of action and reading about it from afar, of which she wrote that 'news [...] which created so much sensation in England, was but little regarded at Spring Hill'.[11]

Mary's first experience of battle was 'pleasant enough', she wrote. After all, this was why she came: to witness and partake in camp life and the pomp, pride and circumstance of glorious war. Sitting on her horse, she enjoyed the amazing sight of English, French and Turkish forces over the plain. How pretty it was to see the clouds of smoke from behind the bushes answered by fire from the other side in skirmishes. 'This was my first experience of actual battle,' she wrote, 'and I felt that strange excitement which I do not remember on future occasions, coupled with an earnest longing to see more of warfare, and to share in its hazards. It was not long before my wish was gratified.'[12]

Mary revelled in danger. All that she had dreamed about was now reality. She was in the midst of it all, although she admitted to knowing very little about the second bombardment of Sebastopol in April. From her position on Spring Hill she was able to judge the severity of the battle by the long trains of wounded that passed by the British Hotel. True to her character, the ever-ready Mary had a stretcher laid near her door, because very often a poor fellow was laid upon it, exhausted by his terrible journey from the field. The bombardment was unsuccessful, and after it, according to Mary, there was a sudden lull in the siege, during which she received a number of visitors including Florence Nightingale, who had come to supervise the Balaclava hospitals. In the wake of the revered Lady of the Lamp, other illustrious people passed Mary's way, such as Monsieur Alexis Soyer, whom Mary described as 'the great high priest of the mysteries of cookery', a regular at Spring Hill.[13] They greeted each other warmly on their first meeting. Soyer described it thus:

As I was not well acquainted with the road across the country, I made up my mind to follow the high one which passes close to headquarters. When about halfway, I perceived a group of officers standing by the roadside round a kind of tent much like a gypsy tent [...] I was riding towards it, when, much to my astonishment, several voices called out – "Soyer! Soyer! Come here – come this way!" I readily complied with the invitation, and found two or three gentlemen whom I had the pleasure of knowing. During our conversation, an old dame of a jovial appearance, but a few shades darker than the white lily, issued from the tent, bawling out, in order to make her voice heard above the noise, "Who is my new son?" to which one of the officers replied, "Monsieur Soyer, to be sure; don't you know him?"

"God bless me, my son, are you Monsieur Soyer of

whom I heard so much in Jamaica? Well, to be sure! I have sold many and many a score of your Relish and other sauces – God knows how many."[14]

Mary invited Soyer to join Sir John Campbell in taking a glass of champagne. As she went to fetch the drink, Campbell explained to Soyer who she was. In turn, Soyer was equally as impressed with the 'celebrated Mrs Seacole' as she was with him. Although Soyer wrote his description of her after the war when she had achieved celebrity status, he gave the impression that she was already a popular figure before her British Hotel fame. Soyer recalled the moment when Mary reappeared with the bottles to treat the gentlemen:

We all declared it would never do for a lady to stand treat in the Crimea.

"Lord bless you, Monsieur Soyer," said the lady, "don't you know me?"

"Yes, I do now, my dear madam."

"Well, all those fine fellows you see here are my Jamaica sons – are you not?" said she, opening the champagne, and addressing the general.

"We are, Mrs Seacole, and a very good mother you have been to us."[15]

They then drank a toast to each other. Mary described the celebrated chef as having 'the most smiling of faces and [wearing] the most gorgeous of irregular uniforms' and wrote that he 'never failed to praise my soups and dainties'. But she fancied herself as a good cook too:

> I always flattered myself that I was his match, and with our West Indian dishes could of course beat him hollow, and more than once I challenged him to a trial of skill; but the gallant Frenchman only shrugged his shoulders, and disclaimed my challenge with many flourishes of his jewelled hands, declaring that Madame proposed a contest where victory would cost him his reputation for gallantry, and be more disastrous than defeat. And all because I was a woman, forsooth.[16]

This kind of talk annoyed Mary, who always spoke up for herself. 'What nonsense,' she wrote, 'to talk like that, when I was doing the work of half a dozen men.'[17] Nonetheless, her sense of humour got the better of her. She, in turn, recognised the Frenchman's good humour and declared that 'when our [Crimean] campaigns were over, we would render rivalry impossible, by combining to open the first restaurant in Europe. There was always fun in the store when the good-natured Frenchman was there.'[18]

Mary's love for, and close association with, soldiers was such that at a moment's notice she was willing to help the first regiment of Sardinian Grenadiers, who stayed at Spring Hill overnight on their way to their positions. By now, it seemed that Mary Seacole's well-founded fear of thievery and thieves had somewhat receded. She was her trusting self again. And fortunately for her and the regiment, not a single item was stolen on the night that they stayed. She marvelled at this all the more because there was no lack of opportunities for the thieves. The war in the Crimea brought many visitors from all over the world to make Spring Hill their headquarters. All sorts of people came and went, and not surprisingly, among them was a 'swindler', a Captain St Clair whom Mary nonetheless treated well. She gave to him the best of everything. Even in such unfortunate circumstances, the goodness of her heart shone through, for she later wrote of him as a man of some substance whom she appreciated. It was this big-heartedness, a capaciousness of spirit and humanity, that set her apart from others in the Crimea. Mary was also re-acquainted with another 'visitor' to the camp in the Crimea: cholera, of which she had had a good deal of experience. Such a visitation at such a time was most unwelcome.

As preparations got under way for the third 'great bombardment' of the city, the summer sunshine broke through beautifully and, for a while, visitors to the Seacole and Day British Hotel were relaxed and cheerful. It was remarkable how quickly moods changed. In this brief period, amusement was the order of the day – races, hunts, cricket matches and dinner parties. As it got hotter, Mary prepared her own popular brand of cooling beverages for friends and customers. The variety of what she presented to the soldiers and officials must have been, apart from taste, most pleasing to the eye. No wonder her sangaree, claret, cider cups and ices went down well! How precious these times were, for soon the bombardment and loss of life would come again. And when it did, it was with renewed and unforgettable ferocity. As she reminded readers of her autobiography, 'although there might be only a few short and sullen roars of the great guns by day, few nights passed without some fighting in the trenches'. The cost was great, and in many cases deeply personal for Mary. 'Very often,' she wrote, 'the news of the morning would be that one or other of those I know had fallen.'[19] This affected her deeply, and often she would wake up in the night hearing the thundering of guns. Day after day, she dreaded the sadness that the dawn would bring. Although bad news was something she had lived with from time to time, it was never easy for her to be the bearer of such news. While Mary went about her business in a cheerful manner, the certainty of death in the trenches haunted her. She explained, 'It was very usual, when a young officer was ordered into the trenches, for him to ride down to Spring Hill to dine, or obtain something more than his ordinary fare to brighten his weary hours in those fearful ditches' – which quickly became graves.[20] Farewells and goodbyes before battles were always poignantly sad reminders of her time in the Crimea. Of the young officers she had known, she wrote:

They seldom failed on these occasions to shake me by the hand at parting, and sometimes would say, "You see, Mrs Seacole, I can't say goodbye to the dear ones at home, so I'll bid you goodbye for them. Perhaps you'll see them some day, and if the Russians should knock me over, mother, just tell them I thought of them all – will you?" And although all this might be said in a lighthearted manner, it was rather solemn. I felt it to be so, for I never failed (although who was I, that I should preach?) to say something about God's providence and relying upon it; and they were very good. No army of parsons could be much better than my sons.[21]

In turn, the men regarded Mary as their 'mother'. She was now known as the 'Mother of the Army'. They were unusually attentive, and as they shook her hand she was overwhelmed by her feelings for them.

She reflected too upon the private soldiers who would often say, 'I'm going in with my Master tonight, Mrs Seacole; come and look after him, if he's hit.'[22] And sure enough, when they left her, she would spend a restless night and an anxious morning waiting for the dreaded news. It had become so personal that she was moved to write, 'I used to think it was like having a large family of children ill with fever, and dreading to hear which one had passed away in the night.'[23] In the aftermath, the dutiful Mary felt bound to go up to the hut of the wounded or sick and do her 'woman's work', to which she was fully committed.

'How could it be otherwise?' she questioned. She remembered the dead and dying faces of many boys and men, including old friends from Jamaica. Reflecting upon these sorrowful occasions, Mary was nevertheless quick to point out that amidst the carnage and suffering, there was little time for grieving. As an eyewitness and participant in the Crimean War, she pointed out that, in relation to 'the horrors of the fatal trenches', the 'real history' had hitherto never been written. But, she added, 'perhaps it is as well that so harrowing a tale should be left in oblivion'. Of those trenches, she told the story of two sergeants, schoolmates who had lost track of each other, until by different routes they met again in, of all places, the trenches, 'under the fire of a common enemy'. When they recognised each other, they raced forward and with a 'hearty handshake' they exchanged mutual greetings. 'While their hands were still clasped,' Mary wrote, 'a chance shot killed both.'[24]

If what she had related above was bad, there was worse to come as she picked her way through the dangerous Crimean battlefield. In a testimonial, the Adjutant-General of the British Army stated that Mary had often done the best she could, 'attending to the wounded men, even in positions of great danger'.[25] Discharging her strong sense of duty, frequently under fire, was paramount to Mary. Danger was endemic in her work and soon, she said, it failed 'to create more than temporary uneasiness'. To illustrate her point, she stated:

Indeed, after Sebastopol was ours, you might often see officers and men strolling coolly, even leisurely, across and along those streets, exposed to the enemy's fire, when a little haste would have carried them beyond the reach of danger. The truth was, I believe, they had grown so habituated to being in peril from shot or shell, that they rather liked the sensation, and found it difficult to get on without a little gratuitous excitement and danger.[26]

At this crucial time of the Crimean campaign, Mary was clearly involved in serious engagements that exposed her to considerable peril. The situation was so risky that one could hardly move around the different camps. At times, the enemy was far too close for comfort. Russian shot had not only struck huts and tents but almost hit Mary too, when on one occasion she was on her horse and a round shot landed almost immediately in front of her.[27]

When eventually the third bombardment of Sebastopol began in the height of summer, the Spring Hill visitors had plenty to talk about. According to Mary, many people guessed when the attack against the Russians would commence. No one doubted the success of this campaign. As planning of the bombardment continued, important secrets oozed out from various places, one of which was the British Hotel. During the run-up to the attack, 'whispers' floated about on Sunday 17 June and 'excited me strangely', Mary admitted. At this strange and momentous time, she explained what happened next:

Any stranger not in my secret would have considered that my conduct fully justified my partner, Mr Day, in sending me home [...] I never remember feeling more excited or more restless than upon that day, and no sooner had night fairly closed in upon us than, instead of making preparations for bed, this same stranger would have seen me wrap up – the nights were still cold – and start off for a long walk to Cathcart's Hill, three miles and a half away. I stayed there until past midnight, but when I returned home, there was no rest for me; for I had found out that, in the stillness of the night, many regiments were marching down to the trenches, and that the dawn of day would be the signal that should let them loose upon the Russians. The few hours still left before daybreak, were made the most of at Spring Hill.[28]

Mary and her helpers prepared for the great onslaught by making cheese sandwiches, packing up fowls, tongues, ham, wine and spirits. She also filled a large bag with lint, bandages, needles, thread and medicines. At daybreak, everything was loaded upon two mules and Mary led the way on horseback. Thus, Mary wrote, 'the little cavalcade left the British Hotel before the sun of the fatal 18th of June had been many hours old.'[29] At this early hour, the cavalry pickets had orders to stop anyone travelling to the scene of action. However, Mary was the sutler extraordinaire and, even at this early hour, the men raised a shout for her. She

wrote that she found Cathcart's Hill crowded with spectators. Carrying provisions to the troops, she learned that
the attack upon the Redan had failed and very wisely went
no further.

But Mary's work was only just beginning, for here she
found plenty of officers, who soon relieved her of her
refreshments, and some wounded men, who found the
contents of her bag useful. After this, she went to assist
doctors at the temporary hospital where she was kept busy
binding up wounds and tending to those who were badly
injured. Throughout the day, Mary came under enemy fire
with worrying regularity. Shot and shell whizzed about,
but Mary was determined to reach those in need of her
bandages and comforts. Mary's dispensation of human
compassion at the risk of her life was rewarded with grateful words and smiles from broken men. Never satisfied,
she pressed on to reach the casualties. It was then that, in
throwing herself to the ground as a shell landed nearby,
she fell heavily on her right thumb and dislocated it. The
thumb never returned to its normal shape. With no water
available, Mary washed her hands with sherry before she
made her way back to Spring Hill, where she was told that
the wayward lad who had accompanied her, either fright-
ened or tired of waiting, had gone away with the mules.
Where to? She mounted her horse and went in search of
the boy. When she found him, some three miles away, she
admits to horsewhipping him, 'the only satisfaction [she]
had'.[30] The tireless Mary moved on with bandages and

refreshments, and at no little risk, to reach the wounded after the attack on General Eyre's division.[31] It was a luckless day, which left many dead. Indeed, the long evening of 18 June was a sad one. Heart-rending news came in of those that had fallen. Mary was deeply upset to hear that two commanders who had been very good to her at Spring Hill had fallen. Among the other glorious dead was a Sir John C— whom she remembered first meeting at her house in Jamaica.

On the following day, 19 June, Mary made her way to the battlefield with dread and anxiety 'to see once more the faces of those who had been so kind to me in life'. The scene, she wrote, was a fearful sight, and she prayed that she would 'never see its like again'.[32] But even as she prayed, she knew it was wishful thinking, because her usefulness in life was directly concerned with scenes of horror and distress. Nonetheless, it took a lot for her to be so horrified. Her feelings were compounded when, in the late afternoon, the Russians handed over the bodies of her two senior officer friends. That moment was an indelible memory. She wrote:

They had stripped Sir John of epaulettes, sword, and boots. Ah! how my heart felt for those at home who would soon hear of this day's fatal work. It was on the following day, I think, that I saw them bury him near Cathcart's Hill, where his tent had been pitched. If I had been in the least humour for what was ludicrous, the looks and curiosity of the Russians who saw me during the armistice would have afforded me considerable amusement. I wonder what rank they assigned me.[33]

The terrors of war were not the only misfortunes that Mary had to endure. Cholera raged around the camps, claiming victims from all ranks. Mary recalled with sorrow a great 'calamity': the death of the 'great soldier' Lord Raglan. She had admired Raglan's 'iron courage, [...] gentle smile and kind word that always show the good man'.[34] Mary knew Lord Raglan well enough and vouched for him being a caring commander. Of all the officers in the British Army, she regarded him as the most forthcoming, an officer who took time to speak to the humblest of his men. Of his last days and following his death, she gave the following insight:

During the time he was ill I was at headquarters several times, and once his servants allowed me to peep into the room where their master lay. I do not think they knew that he was dying, but they seemed very sad and low – far more so than he for whom they feared. And on the day of his funeral I was there again. I never saw such heartfelt gloom as that which brooded on the faces of his attendants; but it was good to hear how they all, even the humblest, had some kind memory of the great general whom Providence had called from his post at such a season of danger and distress. And once again they let me into the room in which the coffin lay, and I timidly stretched out my hand and touched a corner of the union-jack which lay upon it; and then I watched it wind its way through the long lines of soldiery towards Kamiesch, while, ever and anon, the guns thundered forth in sorrow, not in anger. And for days after I could not help thinking of the "Caradoc," which was ploughing its way through the sunny sea with its sad burden.

After these sad events, the mood among the British soldiers began to return more or less to some semblance of its previous state. As Mary put it, 'it was not in the nature of the British army to remain long dull', and soon enough her British Hotel echoed with fun and laughter.[35]

We know a good deal about the horrors and other aspects of the Crimean hostilities, but very little about the business side. How did Mary and Day run the British Hotel? To begin with, the viability of the business warranted regular stock-taking. Several weeks after the battle, the stores of the British Hotel were well filled, and significantly not only with 'every conceivable necessary of life' but also with 'many of its most expensive luxuries'. It was a high point in the hotel's history, and Mary had become the 'Mistress of Spring Hill', who could supply almost anything 'on the spot', or obtain it for you 'if you had a little patience and did not mind a few weeks' delay'.[36] But to manage an establishment such as the British Hotel, Mary had to be responsive to changing conditions. Summertime, for example, brought its own plague of flies. Crimean flies were, in Mary's view, unlike any others, and she hoped such a visitation would not be repeated anywhere else. 'Nature must surely have intended them for blackbeetles,' she noted, 'and accidentally given them wings.'[37] They were a nuisance, hard to exterminate, and it was difficult to escape their attentions either by night or by day. The flies spared no one; all suffered terribly. Mary related the story of a lieutenant, a 'close relative of the Queen' serving in the Royal Naval Brigade, who turned to her for help:

> He evidently considered the fly nuisance the most trying portion of the campaign, and of far more consequence than the Russian shot and shell. "Mami," he said (he had been in the West Indies, and so called me by the familiar term used by the Creole children), "Mami, these flies respect nothing. Not content with eating my prog, they set to at night and make a supper of me," and his face showed traces of their attacks. "Confound them, they'll kill me, Mami; they're everywhere, even in the trenches, and you'd suppose they wouldn't care to go there from choice. What can you do for me, Mami?"[38]

There wasn't very much that Mary could do. But what little she could she did for her royal patient (who is now thought to have been Prince Victor of Hohenlohe-Langenburg, a half-nephew of Queen Victoria).

If she was helpful to others, she was also creative and imaginative in her approach. On one occasion, she remembered riding to a store in Kadikoi, where she bought a piece of muslin which she made into a mosquito net for the prince, who was delighted. When he fell ill later, Mary visited his quarters and gave him all the attention and care she was capable of. As the summer days passed, Mary learned from the guests at the British Hotel that more soldiers had joined the Russian Army, which was preparing for a great battle. By August, the strong rumours became reality with the sound of guns and cannons. Thus the element of surprise was forestalled when at dawn on 16 August heavy firing was heard from the French positions by the Tchernaya River and both troops and spectators poured from all quarters in that direction.

This call to battle found Mary prepared and loaded; soon she was riding towards the scene of action and saw most of it. She witnessed the Russians as they made their way backward and forward across the river. She was near enough to see and hear the Russian officers cheer and wave their men forward in the coolest, bravest manner, just before scores of them were shot down. In the lull between the roars of the guns, she could hear excited cheers, which at times signalled attack and at others repulse. Posterity was blessed by the fact that Mary was well placed to see what the Russians could not. She recalled that the squadrons of English and French cavalry waited 'calmly yet impatiently [...] until the Russians' partial success should

bring their sabres into play'.[39] Though she was unsentimen-
tal, this could not have been easy for Mary. What a resil-
ient woman she was, and what depth of understanding she
showed in this violent man's world. The display of force
was quite impressive, and Mary painted a vivid picture of
the Russians' retreat, writing that 'the dark-plumed Sar-
dinians and red-pantalooned French spread out in pursuit,
and formed a picture so excitingly beautiful that we forgot
the suffering and death they left behind'.

At this stage, she had left her vantage point and had gone
onto the field of battle, where the carnage she witnessed
was unbelievable even by her standards. Bodies lay strewn
on the ground and 'cries of pain' filled the air. Water was
the most precious want, and getting it to the men who were
still alive was an 'errand of mercy' in which many officers
and strangers engaged. Although the Russian guns were
still firing, plunderers, especially the French, searched and
stripped the dead of what was valuable, paying no regard to
'the presence of a lady'. Such hasty, indecent behaviour did
not meet Mary's approval. Her spirited complaints (true
to character) were met with laughter, which she ignored.
By contrast, she was more charitable, patching up not only
French and Sardinian soldiers but also the Russian sick
and wounded. Intrepid as ever, she proceeded to examine
the shattered bodies before her and try to help them.

One Russian soldier was so badly wounded in the lower
jaw as to put him beyond repair, she recalled. Yet she tried
to dislodge a musket ball in his mouth. In a reflex action,

he bit so hard as to leave a permanent scar on Mary's finger. Before this patient finally died, Mary recorded that his features had softened and 'a smile spread over his rough inexpressive face'.[40] No death left Mary unaffected, and now she shifted her attention to another fallen Russian, an officer who was shot in the side. She watched him bear his pain with noble fortitude. As if to compensate for the wordless passing of his comrade, this second Russian, unable to speak English, was more demonstrative of his gratitude for her kindness.

Mary always had a ready, genuine smile for others, and its value in the Crimea at this time was never greater. There were many to whom she gave her close attention, and it was fortunate that her warm, expressive, motherly face was the last that many soldiers saw. Giving was, it seemed, even for this pragmatic woman, better than receiving. Doing, being useful, was its own reward. Mementos, however, even relating to war, had their own value, all the more for Mary, who was an 'actor' in the field of battle. While she found the idea of robbing either the living or the dead abhorrent, she could not resist snapping up some souvenirs: a few buttons from the coats of dead soldiers.

8

Aftermath

Less than a month after the battle of the Tchernaya, Mary experienced her busiest and most eventful few weeks. Paradoxically, it was at a time when there was not much happening at Spring Hill. It was the calm before the big storm: the last bombardment of Sebastopol. In her autobiography, Mary set the scene:

> Every one was either at his post, or too anxiously await-
> ing the issue of the last great bombardment to spend
> much time at the British Hotel. I think that I lost more
> of my patients and customers during those few weeks
> than during the whole previous progress of the siege.
> Scarce a night passed that I was not lulled to sleep
> with the heavy continuous roar of the artillery; scarce
> a morning dawned that the same sound did not usher
> in my day's work. The ear grew so accustomed during
> those weeks to the terrible roar that when Sebastopol
> fell the sudden quiet seemed unnatural and made
> us dull. And during the whole of this time the most

perplexing rumours flew about, some having reference to the day of assault, the majority relative to the last great effort which it was supposed the Russians would make to drive us into the sea. I confess these latter rumours now and then caused me temporary uneasiness, Spring Hill being on the direct line of route which the actors in such a tragedy must take.[1]

Mary spent a good deal of her time on Cathcart's Hill. Her 'curiosity and excitement' for war had not waned. In fact, it was aroused by the ongoing horrendous bombardment. She was anxious to get closer. Almost casually, at this juncture in her autobiography she wrote about the shells that 'now and then [...] would fall among the crowd of onlookers'.[2] Surprisingly, such danger did not disturb either Mary or the ghoulish visitors, whose sense of excitement and expectation far outweighed the danger of being killed.

Such bravery as was shown by Mary and the spectators was, it seemed, matched by a ceremony that was held amidst the shelling. This was the moment chosen to honour a select few with the Order of the Bath. For Mary, who was always on the go, this was a time to stop, a moment to which she was proud to bear witness. As she put it, 'although it cost me a day, I considered that I had fairly earned the pleasure.'[3] She felt a sense of deep personal satisfaction, and for the occasion she baked a cake which was dressed up with bright banners and flags. Mary acknowledged that she 'received great kindness from the officials at the ceremony, and from the officers [...] who recognised [her]'.[4] A few days after the ceremony, the ongoing bombardment had become so fearful that Mary thought the end of the world was at hand. The city was pounded with, it seemed, every shot and shell. She gave an account of what happened next during this action:

> The firing began at early dawn, and was fearful. Sleep was impossible; so I arose, and set out for my old station on Cathcart's Hill. And here, with refreshments for the anxious lookers-on, I spent most of my time, right glad of any excuse to witness the last scene of the siege. It was from this spot that I saw fire after fire break out in Sebastopol, and watched all night the beautiful yet terrible effect of a great ship blazing in the harbour, and lighting up the adjoining country for miles.[5]

On the morning of 8 September, the capricious Crimean weather changed again: it became cold and wintry. And as she had done on the terrible 18 June, Mary anticipated a catastrophe. Early that morning, she was already on her horse, laden with necessary supplies. Once again she encountered sentries who were posted to deter onlookers from progressing further. Her reputation had, however, preceded her, and now it served as her passport, as the officers relaxed the rule in her favour. Having made this journey so often, Mary found herself once more at an early hour in her familiar spot with her tried-and-tested medicines, bandages and drinks for the wounded and fatigued. What she did not expect was that the disastrous consequences of the day would so closely approximate the losses of the last attack.

After the incessant din of the morning's battle, suddenly at midday the cannonade ceased, and from her vantage point Mary saw an almost unbelievable sight. The Malak-hoff redoubt had been taken by the French, but the British assault on the Redan had failed. She proceeded to attend to the large number of wounded, among whom were many officers of her beloved 97th Regiment, whom she had known in Jamaica. Their losses were terrible. Engrossed in her care of the wounded, she was careless of her own safety as shells fell here and there. Luckily, she escaped injury when a shell fell so close as to make her seriously fright-ened. Nonetheless, she took home a fragment of the huge shell as a souvenir.

Despite this brush with injury or even death, Mary was a conspicuous figure on the battlefield, applying herself with selfless diligence. At this awful time, Mary was spotted by the correspondent for *The Times* William Howard Russell, whom she had often spotted taking down notes and sketches of the scene, under fire.[6] This was to be the occasion when the keen-eyed correspond-ent made Mary Seacole a household name. He was the first war correspondent, and his reports from the Crimea were hugely influential with the British public. (Inciden-tally, Roger Fenton was recognised as the first British war photographer because of his work in the Crimea, but the title of the first war photographer must go to Carol Szathmari, who also photographed the Crimean War. William Simpson became the celebrated British artist of the Crimean War, and writers such as Tolstoy, Tennyson and Dickens have made reference to the conflict.)

If Mary was little known in England hitherto, Russell was now ready to lift her from obscurity and put her centre stage by informing the readers of *The Times*:

> I have seen her go down, under fire, with her little store of creature comforts for our wounded men; and a more tender or skilful hand about a wound or broken limb could not be found among our best surgeons. I saw her at the assault on the Redan, at the Tchernaya, at the fall of Sebastopol, laden, not with plunder, good old soul! but with wine, bandages, and food for the wounded or the prisoners.[7]

Mary laboured among the fallen men all day and stayed on Cathcart's Hill late into the night. She watched, awe-struck, as Sebastopol burned. The chill wind made her shiver as she approached Spring Hill. She had a sleepless night which was lit up by the glare of the burning city. Mary believed that, unlike herself, the weary soldiers slept soundly even through the terrible night of the final assault. In fact, those who could and did sleep woke up to find Sebastopol deserted to its victors, 'a heap of ruins', and before noon the following day no one but dead and dying Russians was in the south side of the famous and once beautiful city.

At last, there came the good news that the Russians were to evacuate Sebastopol. This had the effect of dispelling most of the tiredness of the previous days. For Mary's part, there was a challenge to be met: she offered bets that she would be the first woman from the English lines to enter the fallen city. Although she needed an official pass to enter, when she did so, she was, predictably, carrying refreshments. Once more her reputation and her good works got her through. But as she passed the sentries, those officers who had not been given passes did not hide their annoyance at being thwarted from entering Sebastopol.

Mary recalled riding through the city, many parts of which were still ablaze. Explosions here and there added to the dangers. Nonetheless, curiosity and excitement drove her on. She stopped often to attend to officers and men in need of refreshments and attention. A few had acquainted themselves with Russian wine cellars and were 'ingloriously drunk' when Mary reached them. This was an attractive option for the vanquished also, who were faced with the choice between memory and forgetting. Here too Mary was offered, and took, many trophies, including a gaily decorated altar-candle studded with gold and silver stars, an old cracked china teapot, a cracked bell and a parasol. Whilst collecting these items, she never forgot that she was in the fearful city that had caused so much death and suffering. As she passed along the streets, amid many hazards, she was increasingly aware of being exposed to Russian fire. In spite of their watchfulness, some in her entourage narrowly escaped being hit. Further into the city, the dangers were more apparent as fires broke out all around her, while mines exploded without warning. With great difficulty, Mary and her companions succeeded in getting into the part of Sebastopol held by the French. Here, she nearly got into serious trouble. While inspecting the ruins and observing some Frenchmen plundering a house, she was accused by a young American sailor of being a Russian spy. Predictably, she was incensed by the audacious charge and refused to dismount her horse. Instead, she used her bell to hit the first soldier who tried to lay hands on her, which made the Frenchmen more determined to arrest Mary. They attempted to manhandle her into a guardhouse. Mary resisted and screamed for help. Just then, a French officer whom she had treated as a patient at Spring Hill after the battle of the Tchernaya appeared and wasted no time in ordering Mary's release. But this was not quite the end of the matter. Immediately after, Mary (now 51 years old) flew at the American who had caused the trouble. She used her bell, and her companions wielded their riding whips, to inflict what she felt was just punishment.

After the French soldiers' apologies to Mary, she acquired another 'trophy' of incalculable value while on the way back to Spring Hill. It was a picture of the Madonna, some

eight or ten feet in length, which had been cut from above
the altar of a church in Sebastopol. Mary was not very religious, but she was appreciative of those who were believ-
ers. Fundamentally, she was a passionate humanitarian, a
doer, rather than a preacher or congregant. Nonetheless,
she was appreciative of the image she had brought home:

> I am no judge of such things, but I think, although the
> painting is rather coarse, that the face of the Virgin, and
> the heads of the cherubim that fill the cloud from which
> she is descending, are soft and beautiful. There is a look
> of divine calmness and heavenly love in the Madonna's
> face which is very striking; and, perhaps, during the
> long and awful siege many a knee was bent in worship
> before it, and many a heart found comfort in its soft
> loving gaze.

The next day Mary went back to Sebastopol, where her
exploration led her to yet more of the city's horrors. Suffice
it to say that she found there a woeful hospital where
thousands of dead and dying had been left by the retreat-
ing Russians, which was enough to unnerve the strong-
est and sicken the most experienced.[8] This was perhaps
the most harrowing sight she had ever seen. Thereafter,
dutiful Mary also returned to the Redan, where at every
turn there was still danger. She noted the 'houses' opened
by some French women in Sebastopol, but she was not
tempted to do the same. She was content to see through

the Crimean campaign from her war-seasoned old quarters at Spring Hill.

At last, the Crimean campaign was over and the 'great work', as Mary called it, was accomplished. The Russians had retired, and a novel position existed. The questions Mary and others then posed were: what was to be done? And was there to be more fighting? The answers to such questions were, of course, in the hands of the strategists at the British headquarters and their leaders at home.

While deliberations continued, the soldiers diverted their attention to amusements with 'the same energy and activity which had made Sebastopol a heap of ruins and a well-filled cemetery'. Now they were 'set to work as eager to kill their present enemy, Time, as they had lately been to destroy their fled enemies, the Russians'.[9] The fear and terror of the battle for Sebastopol in the summer was followed by what in Mary's words was a 'beautiful autumn', which preceded the second winter of the Crimean campaign. The survivors felt they had earned the right to some relaxation and enjoyment. How much more could those who survived the war take? Not surprisingly, the pendulum of human endurance had now swung the other way as a carnival spirit infected the visitors, officers and men. Life was short, and pleasure was not an option for too long. But now, Mary wrote, it was 'hunted keenly'. It was to be had in sports, pastimes, theatricals, parties and, of course, dinners. Mary's dinner parties included men of high rank such as the Duc de Rouchefoucauld, a prince of the French imperial family, and Viscount Talon. Many attested to the quality of her cooking.[10]

It was clear that now, after the fall of Sebastopol, Mary was more amenable to the French, and in doing her best for them, she learned a great deal. Her verdict on them was, 'It is true that they carried from Sebastopol the lion's share of glory. My belief is that they deserved it, having borne by far a larger proportion of suffering.'[11] While Mary basked in the high praise she received for her dinners at Spring Hill, one wonders whether she, in turn, complimented her unsung, devoted black cook and other helpers. Understandably, she was the one to whom attention was directed. Toasts were drunk to her good health. The French prince paid several visits to the British Hotel. She revelled in the activities of the higher classes. At this time, and in such grand company, Mary spoke of hunting in the Crimea and said her experience of Crimean horse races was perfect. The 'sport of kings' was held several times around Christmas, and these were events of great interest. Mary attended the meetings, and was better prepared with each one. She was struck by how well the managers of these Crimean races replicated 'the old familiar scenes at home'.[12] Things had improved markedly after the earlier shortages and mismanagement in the camps; communications with England were far better now than they had been when Mary first arrived in the Crimea. This was reflected in the high quality of racing gear that was assembled: racing saddles, boots, silk caps and jackets. Mary also observed that some soldiers put on blackface and came out caricaturing Ethiopian serenaders, as if anticipating the well-known African tipster and showman of the 1960s, Prince Monolulu – although it would puzzle the most ingenious to guess where they got their wigs and banjos from.

How odd that against a setting of such fear – the terror of battles past and the foreboding of those to come – there should be a show of normal life. A few weeks before Christmas, there was a great explosion in the French ammunition dump, in which many were killed. This led to friction between French and British soldiers over the two armies' relative performances at the Malakhoff and the Redan respectively. There was also at this time a rare occurrence: Mary fell ill, for the first and only time in the Crimea. Considering her proximity to sickness and disease, from Cruces to the Crimea, one is struck by the extraordinary physical and mental constitution she possessed. Nonetheless, her illness was not of much consequence, and she attributed it to a sudden cold snap that had taken her by surprise. During this lapse in health, apart from the kindness of her soldier friends, she also received much sympathy and many presents such as warm clothing, but she wrote that 'the most delicate piece of attention was shown me by one of the Sappers and Miners, who, hearing the report that I was dead, positively came down to Spring Hill to take my measure for a coffin'.[13] Rather than be offended, Mary felt flattered, touched by such thoughtful attention (could she ever have too much attention?).

When Christmas eventually came, it was with pleasant memories of home and 'home comforts'. Mary was also cheered by news from abroad which reflected her growing reputation in the Crimea. One of her greetings read:

A merry Christmas to you [...] and many of them. Although you will not write to us, we see your name frequently in the newspapers, from which we judge that you are strong and hearty. All your old Jamaica friends are delighted to hear of you, and say that you are an honour to the Isle of Springs.[14]

Mary's pro-British stance had served her well, and now at Christmas she did the English thing as hostess of the British Hotel. She planned to serve plum pudding and mince pies. It was a Christmas which she hoped her 'sons' would never forget, and 'For three weeks previous to Christmas-day,' she wrote, 'my time was fully occupied in making preparations for it.'[15] The thought that this could well be the soldiers' last Christmas gave the occasion added significance. While it meant hard work for the great organiser and proprietor of the British Hotel, it was a magnet for Britons who eagerly anticipated her wholesome and exotic cooking. Mary rose to the task and her Christmas fare was a huge success, so much so that one customer referring to an order for mince pies for a certain captain said, 'Sure, he likes them well done, ma'am. Bake 'em as brown as your own purty face, darlint.'[16] This reference to her race did not escape Mary's attention – hence its inclusion in her autobiography. After many hours of preparation and cooking, all that Mary had intended to offer her customers and friends was served up, and all were duly satisfied by her Herculean efforts. But what about her own Christmas dinner? Rules were rules and, as Mary said, she had to wait until eight o'clock before she could sit down to dinner.

Then New Year's Day brought its own demands for pies and puddings, and reminded Mary's patients of the home comforts for which they longed. One patient in particular caught Mary's attention and left an indelible impression. He 'had been a most industrious and honest fellow' whom Mary found very weak and ill. She stayed with him for quite a while and noted:

> [...] before I left him, kind fancy had brought to his bedside his wife and children from his village-home in England, and I could hear him talking to them in a low and joyful tone. Poor, poor fellow! the New Year so full of hope and happiness had dawned upon him, but he did not live to see the wild flowers spring up peacefully through the war-trodden sod before Sebastopol.[17]

So ended the memorable Christmas and New Year celebrations at the British Hotel.

With the first days of the New Year, the prospects of reaching a peaceful settlement and of going home were uppermost in the minds of the officers, the soldiers and

Mary, even though the consequences, as we shall see, were unfavourable to her. Everyone had had enough, and they waited for news of the cessation of hostilities, which was not long in coming. Before the armistice was signed, Mary noted there were instances of closer relations and advances of friendship between the Russians and their adversaries. Thus foes became friends, and the banks of the Tchernaya were the setting for a strange camaraderie. Mary, who was among the first to visit Tchernaya, wrote how 'very much delighted seemed the Russians to see an English woman' – another indication that she identified with Britishness so strongly that she had no idea of being Jamaican (Jamaica being a British colony then anyway). She went on to write, 'I wonder if [the Russians] thought that [the English] all had my complexion.'[18] The colour of her skin had not deterred her before, and it was not going to do so now. She soon fell in with the current amusement of swapping coins with the Russians.

After this interlude of exchange and camaraderie came the last shots of any consequence. They signalled the final moments of hostilities and ushered in the good news of peace. Soon after, Mary wrote, the home-going began, accompanied by 'happy faces and light hearts, and some kind thoughts and warm tears for the comrades left behind'.[19] Mary was 'very glad to hear of peace', but since war was profitable the peace came at a price. As she rightly felt, everyone who had used her hotel was aware that peace would cause her 'ruin'. The Crimean War and the British

Hotel were inseparable, both conceptually and practically. In her autobiography Mary recalled the magnitude of what she now faced:

> We had lately made extensive additions to our store and outhouses – our shelves were filled with articles laid in at a great cost, and which were now unsaleable, and which it would be equally impossible to carry home. Everything, from our stud of horses and mules down to our latest consignments from home, must be sold for any price; and, as it happened, for many things, worth a year ago their weight in gold, no purchaser could now be found.[20]

Not long after the war, the firm of Seacole and Day would be declared bankrupt. Depressing as her thoughts about her business prospects were, before leaving the Crimea, Mary decided to see more of the hinterland. In Bakhchysarai she had an amusing and pleasant time, even though her hungry companions had to forego food in a hamper in which they discovered a rat. The last peaceful days of winter gave way to spring, and Mary touchingly recorded the scene of the troops' orderly departure:

> As they passed the Iron House [the British Hotel] where so much of life's action had been compressed into so short a space of time – they would stop and give us a parting cheer, while very often the band struck up some

familiar tune of that home they were so gladly seeking. And very often the kind-hearted officers would find time to run into the British Hotel to bid us goodbye, and give us a farewell shake of the hand; for you see war, like death, is a great leveller, and mutual suffering and endurance had made us all friends.[21]

Wise words from a veteran. Mary kept many letters and scribblings from this time of parting, one of which read, 'My dear Mrs. Seacole, and my dear Mr. Day, [...] I have called here four times this day, to wish you good-bye. I am so sorry I was not fortunate enough to see you. I shall still hope to see you tomorrow morning. We march at seven a.m.'[22]

Despite her apparent composure at this time, the to-ing and fro-ing of departure from the Crimea all seemed 'strange and somewhat sad' to Mary. In a revealing and quite understandable passage, she wrote:

[...] sometimes I felt that I could not sympathise with the glad faces and happy hearts of those who were looking forward to the delights of home, and the joy of seeing once more the old familiar faces remembered so fondly in the fearful trenches and the hard-fought battlefields. Now and then we would see a lounger with a blank face, taking no interest in the bustle of departure, and with him I acknowledged to have more fellow-feeling than with the others, for he, as well as I, clearly had no home to go to. He was soldier by choice and necessity, as well as by profession. He had no home, no loved friends; the peace would bring no particular pleasure to him, whereas war and action were necessary to his existence, gave him excitement, occupation, the chance of promotion. Now and then, but seldom, however, you came across such a disappointed one. Was it not so with me? Had I not been happy through the months of toil and danger, never knowing what fear or depression was, finding every moment of the day mortgaged hours in advance, and earning sound sleep and contentment by sheer hard work? What better or happier lot could possibly befall me? And, alas! how likely was it that my present occupation gone, I might long in vain for another so stirring and so useful. Besides which, it was pretty sure that I should go to England poorer than I left it, and although I was not ashamed of poverty; beginning life again in the autumn – I mean late in the summer of life – is hard uphill work.[23]

Then came the moment of her own Crimean farewell. She left with many testimonials to her devoted work in the Crimea, and she distinguished between those she received from officers and those from the enlisted men. She preferred the thoughts and letters from members of the latter group, and inserted one written on 16 June 1856 into her autobiography:

My Dear Mrs Seacole – As you are about to leave the Crimea, I avail myself of the only opportunity which may occur for some time, to acknowledge my gratitude to you, and to thank you for the kindness which I, in common with many others, received at your hands, when attacked with cholera in the spring of 1855. But I have no language to do it suitably.

I am truly sensible that your kindness far exceeded my claims upon your sympathy. It is said by some of your friends, I hope truly, that you are going to England. There can be none from the Crimea more welcome there, for your kindness in the sick-tent, and your heroism in the battle-field, have endeared you to the whole army.

I am sure when her most gracious Majesty the Queen shall have become acquainted with the service you have gratuitously rendered to so many of her brave soldiers, her generous heart will thank you. For you have been an instrument in the hands of the Almighty to preserve many a gallant heart to the empire, to fight and win her battles, if ever again war may become a necessity. Please to accept this from your most grateful humble servant, W. J. Tynan.[24]

9

Last Years: Crimean Heroine

Mary arrived back in England in August 1856. A few days later, she attended a public banquet in Kennington. The occasion was to honour those who served in the Crimea. It was a huge celebration attended by 2,000 troops packed into the Royal Surrey Gardens.[1] A *News of the World* reporter wrote:

> Immediately behind the chair in front of the orchestra was a very handsome trophy of flags and laurel wreaths, with Redan and Malakhoff inscribed on each side and Miss Nightingale's name in the centre [...] among the fair visitors in the upper side gallery [where uninvited guests sat] was Mrs Seacole, whose dark features were quite radiant with delight and good humour as she gazed on the pleasant scene below.[2]

The Times, on the other hand, stated:

> [...] among the illustrious [onlookers] was Mrs Seacole,

whose appearance awakened the most rapturous enthusiasm. The soldiers not only cheered her, but chaired
her around the gardens, and she really might have suffered from the oppressive attentions of her admirers,
were it not that two sergeants of extraordinary stature
gallantly undertook to protect her from the pressure of
the crowd.[3]

While Mary was being uproariously acclaimed in
public, Florence Nightingale, that other Crimean heroine,
opted for seclusion.[4] Put simply, Mary loved publicity
and thrived on it, while Florence did not. After this event,
Mary returned to Aldershot, where she was staying, but by
October she was in London, where she lived at 1 Tavistock
Street, near Drury Lane and Covent Garden. In her rented
room she lived modestly. Money was in short supply, but
there was an abundance of well-wishers and friends from
whom she received a good deal of moral support during
the period when the Seacole and Day business was bankrupt. Eventually, when a settlement was reached in court,
the judge awarded Day and Mary an allowance of two
guineas each.[5] Two weeks later, a letter was published in
The Times reminding readers of Mary's sterling service in
the Crimea and the importance of 'acts of benevolence' at
this time of need. The writer proposed a donation of £20,
and asked others to join him. Further correspondence
resulted in pledges of money, and *Punch* chimed in:

Dame Seacole was a kindly old soul,
And a kindly old soul was she;
You might call for your pot, you might call for your pipe,
In her tent on "the Col" so free
[...]
And now the good soul is "in the hole,"
What red-coat in all the land,
But to set her upon her legs again
Will not lend a willing hand?[6]

Early the next year, the firm of Seacole and Day was legally free to operate again, and Mary felt a new lease of life. But thoughts of the war were never far from her mind – all the more so because she was never formally awarded any of the Crimean campaign medals that she wore during the earlier court hearings. There is no record that she ever received an award, as biographer Jane Robinson has written:

It is more than likely that Mary "distinguished" herself. Miniatures were obtained by her army friends, or bought on the open market, and [...] she resolved to wear them, by right to commemorate the fallen and in recognition of her commitment to the British cause. Miniatures are not real medals: they're items of jewellery. But what they signified to Mary went far beyond an ornament.[7]

At the time, many eyewitness accounts of the Crimean

War were being published, and the publisher James Black-wood commissioned Mary to write her memoir, *Wonder-ful Adventures of Mrs Seacole in Many Lands*. The book was helped by William Howard Russell's endorsement, which appears at the beginning:

> I should have thought that no preface would have been required to introduce Mrs. Seacole to the British public, or to recommend a book which must, from the circumstances in which the subject of it was placed, be unique in literature. If singleness of heart, true charity, and Christian works; if trials and sufferings, dangers and perils, encountered boldly by a helpless woman on her errand of mercy in the camp and in the battlefield, can excite sympathy or move curiosity, Mary Seacole will have many friends and many readers. She is no Anna Comnena, who presents us with a verbose history, but a plain truth-speaking woman, who has lived an adventurous life amid scenes which have never yet found a historian among the actors on the stage where they passed. I have witnessed her devotion and courage; I have already borne testimony to her services to all who needed them. She is the first who has redeemed the name of "sutler" from the suspicion of worthlessness, mercenary baseness, and plunder; and I trust that England will not forget one who nursed her sick, who sought out her wounded to aid and succour them, and who performed the last offices for some of her illustrious dead.[8]

In the meantime, Mary's circumstances had not improved and were becoming increasingly, embarrassingly evident. She urgently needed money. Fortunately, a subscription fund was officially set up and a committee of trustees was established. To achieve their objective, a series of fundraising concerts to be held in the Royal Surrey Gardens was planned. Finally, in July 1857, Mary's *Wonderful Adventures* was published. Robinson has described the book thus:

> [It is] part autobiography, part travelogue, not to raise the profile of Afro-Caribbeans or women, but of [Mary] herself. It is neither a political statement nor an artistic exercise; it's a glorious advertisement, written by a celebrity fully in control of her own image. What disturbs many modern readers most about the book is Mary's refusal to identify more fully with her African heritage.[9]

Nonetheless, the book was successful. The first print run was sold within eight months, and the book was reissued in March 1858. What perhaps prevented the book from enjoying even greater success was the fact that the Indian Rebellion flared up just prior to its publication, and news reached London of the massacre of British men in Meerut, India. The perceived savagery of the dark-skinned rebels caused revulsion among the white British populace, and may have affected demand for Mary's book. Nonetheless,

Wonderful Adventures did Mary Seacole proud, and the Royal Surrey Gardens concerts drew large crowds. However, Mary only received £57, which was nowhere near enough assistance.

Sometime between 1859 and 1860 Mary returned to Jamaica, and soon afterward she heard of the death of her friend and fellow cook, Alexis Soyer. While she was on the island a political demonstration in Morant Bay resulted in the local militia firing at the crowd, killing 28 people, on the orders of Governor Edward John Eyre. The British public was shocked, and Eyre was recalled to London. Thereafter, Jamaica's House of Assembly was replaced by Crown colony government, administered directly by Britain. Subsequently, Mary became a direct beneficiary of this approach, and the Seacole Fund was re-established in London in 1867. With donations coming in from high-profile individuals and royalty, including the queen, Mary's financial position improved.

By 1870, Mary, now in her 65th year, looked suitably venerable and was highly regarded by a cross-section of British society. Upon the outbreak of the Franco-Prussian War, Mary was, unsurprisingly, ready once more with her medicine kit to travel to the aid of soldiers in need. She duly applied to be of service, but she was not allowed to go because officials felt she was too much of a national asset to lose. Her disappointment can only be imagined. However, what has survived from that time is a letter from Florence Nightingale to her brother-in-law, the politician

Sir Harry Verney, dated 5 August 1870 and marked 'Burn':

Mrs Seacole.

I dare say you know more about her than I do.

She kept – I will not call it a "bad house" but something not unlike it – in the Crimean War.

She was very kind to the men & what is more, to the Officers – & did some good – & made many drunk.

(A shameful ignorant imposture was practised on the Queen who subscribed to the "Seacole Testimonial.")

I had the greatest difficulty in repelling Mrs Seacole's advances, & in preventing association between her & my nurses (absolutely out of the question) when we established 2 hospitals nursed by us between Kadikoi & the "Seacole Establishment" (in the Crimea).

But I was successful – without any open collision with Mrs Seacole – which I was anxious to avoid – (You will understand that any "rivalry" between the "Seacole" & the "Nightingale" "Establishment(s)" was very much to be averted)

Any one who employs Mrs. Seacole will introduce much kindness – also much drunkenness & improper conduct, wherever she is.

She had then, however, one or more "persons" with her, whom (I conclude) she has not now. I conclude (& believe) that respectable Officers were entirely ignorant of what I... could not help knowing as a Matron & Chaperone & Mother of the Army.[10]

If this harsh judgement hints at more than a whiff of jealousy, there was more to come from the revered Lady with the Lamp, who, unlike Mary, was granted an audience with the queen. Why? Nightingale was the British establishment's own home-grown Crimean heroine. Mary was a colonial subject and, in spite of her fame, she was perceived by many as being very unusual, un-English in her bearing and manner, and therefore on the periphery of the British public's consciousness. Nightingale, in spite of the revered place she held in the heart of the nation, was nevertheless jealous of Mary's celebrity. She was determined to push Mary out of the limelight and, worse, even to besmirch her reputation. An article in *History Today* cites a number of reasons why Mary was never invited to meet Queen Victoria, including the charges contained in the above-mentioned letter that Mary had served alcohol to officers and men, that she pleaded poverty when she shouldn't and, scandalously, that a young woman known as Sally – who was present in the Crimea and who, like everyone else, called Mary 'Mother' – was in fact her illegitimate daughter.[11]

On this controversial matter of Sally being Mary's illegitimate child, Nightingale pointed the finger of suspicion at Colonel Henry Bunbury for being the father.[12] This may not be true, for no evidence has been produced to support it. But the question of Sally's paternity is an intriguing one. Given that in her autobiography Mary was economical with the truth about her early life in Jamaica, if Sally was Mary's daughter it is more than likely that her father would have been someone whom Mary knew well and trusted. She mentioned such a person, someone with whom she had a long and close association, often in her writing. And judging from the tone of her words, Mary respected this person more than any other. The man I refer to is Thomas Day, the Englishman and later business partner whom Mary had met in Jamaica. He may well have known Mary at the time of her marriage to Edwin Seacole, who was in very poor health throughout the marriage. The business, a store, that Mary and Edwin had set up in Black River had to be abandoned and, as mentioned earlier, Edwin died soon after their return to Kingston. As far as we know, the Seacoles had no children. Nonetheless, Mary's association with Day seemed to become closer, for they were both attracted to business ventures, as was Edwin. But, unlike the sickly Edwin, Day was a robust entrepreneur. We first hear of Day in Mary's autobiography, where she stated that he invited her to Navy Bay. 'He was a distant connection of my late husband,' she wrote, 'and treated me with great kindness.' [13]

Researchers have explained that Mary left Jamaica for Central America because of the many proposals of marriage she had been receiving. But she withstood all their attentions, saying she was confident enough to remain an unprotected female. But while marriage was out of the question, we do not know that she was against a relationship. Fully in control of how she remembered and wrote her story, Mary placed Day in Escribanos (Navy Bay), Central America, where they met, thus dispelling the argument that she was escaping the attentions of the opposite sex. Day was there on business relating to mines and gold-prospecting. Interestingly, before she went to meet Day she had already heard about the conflict in the Crimea and Britain's growing interest and involvement. In fact, war seemed inevitable, and when she and Day met in Escribanos, they may well have discussed the subject of Mary's ambition of going to the war zone to help her wounded 'sons'.

After she failed to be taken on as a nurse in London, she again met Day. Was it the chance meeting that Mary made it out to be, or did they plan to meet there? In her autobiography, she wrote that while her 'new scheme [namely, opening a hotel for invalids] was maturing',[14] and after meeting Day, she decided to pay her way to the Crimea. But, she speculated, 'My funds, although they might, carefully husbanded, carry me over the three thousand miles, and land me at Balaclava, would not support me there long.'[15] How much more than her passage money did she have? Did her friend Day help? It is more than likely that he did, because as Mary tells us, he too was heading in the same direction on shipping business, which would have been music to Mary's ears. So far, a pattern begins to emerge in their relationship, and one is tempted to ask: were their meetings fortuitous or planned? From London, she was ready to follow Day on to Balaclava, where she anticipated his letters.

Eventually, on Mary's arrival in the Crimea, she and Day as 'partners' engaged in the incredible undertaking of establishing their Seacole and Day British Hotel. It was a historic coming together of Mary and her friend on a project that would catapult Mary to public prominence; to get it off the ground, a large capital outlay was needed. How much money did Mary have at this time? We have no answer to this question. All she admits to is that the hotel cost 'no less' than £800. Was this an underestimate? From here on, Day was always around, close to hand, supervising and giving Mary advice even about her own safety. Judging from her autobiography, Day was Mary's silent, but crucially close, partner – which should not detract from the fact that she was indeed the colourful lady ambassador, the one who brought the enterprise alive.

Then, as the war raged on about them, Sally showed up at the British Hotel and gossip and comments came from visitors such as Soyer and Nightingale. Both were astonished to see the handsome teenage girl with brown skin and blue eyes. Florence thought she was the daughter of a Mr Bunbury. If Sally was fourteen, then her birth in Jamaica would have been sometime around 1841, when both Mary and Day were in Jamaica. Mary has said that Sally was not her daughter. Nonetheless, her relationship with Day remained paramount, for finally, at the end of the bloody war, they consoled each other over their losses, not only of stock but also of their British Hotel. On their return to England, Mary and Day were together again in

Aldershot, where together they faced bankruptcy until they were both adjudged legally free to practise in business once more. It is clear that Day played a key role in helping Mary to realise her visionary Crimean scheme. She knew him well enough before and after her husband's death and then into her old age, but although the Crimean heroine has provided us with the clues, no one has hitherto recognised or detailed Mary Seacole's close, crucial and enduring relationship with Day.

Given that Victorian Britain was securely founded upon a combination of race, class and colour, it was incredible that Mary got as far as she did. This, in large part, also helps to explain why Nightingale was allowed to reign supreme. Even at the height of Mary's fame, and although the British press had praised Mary in the post-war euphoria, they paid respect where it was due, but nothing more. And when the Crimean troops of all ranks who knew and loved Mary had passed away, her reputation among the living seemed to die too. Fortunately, she enjoyed a wide circle of friends, and proudly wore her 'medals'. By 1876, at the age of 71, she was living free of debt and much more easily, at 26 Upper George Street. It was time for her to make her will, and five years later she changed address again to 3 Cambridge Street. For this intrepid traveller, it was to be her last move. She died in May 1881 and left an estate worth £2,615. 11s. 7d, a huge sum at the time.[16]

Mary was buried in St Mary's Roman Catholic Cemetery in Kensal Green, and was quickly forgotten. Then,

67 years after her death, a shipload of Jamaicans arrived at Tilbury Docks aboard the appropriately named *SS Empire Windrush*, heralding an influx of Commonwealth migrants – including a number of qualified and trainee nurses. Although Mary Seacole was the 19th-century precursor of these 20th-century Caribbean nurses, few of them, if any, knew who she was. With continued migration and settlement in the post-1950 era, the children of the empire and their descendants in Britain engaged in struggles of race, class and colour, and began to assert their identities and claim their heritage. There was a thirst for knowledge, and researchers abounded. Thus history and culture came into play, and new research revealed the hidden histories of heroic figures including Mary Seacole. In 1973, her memory was restored with a ceremony at her graveside, and in 2004, she was voted the 'Greatest Black Briton'. So, 148 years later, in post-empire Britain, Mary Seacole's reputation is greater than it was in 1856. Tirelessly remedying ills on three continents, she was truly international, a one-off, ahead of her time. In recognition of her heroic struggles, the Jamaican government awarded their Order of Merit to her in 1990. And, as if in recognition of these developments, a long-lost portrait of her, an oil painting by Albert Charles Challen, was rediscovered in 2005.

Whether or not Mary was the greatest black Briton, few could doubt the happiness and pride with which she demonstrated her Britishness. But while the particularity of her race is important, it was her enduring goodness of heart that is the hallmark of her greatness. As an individual, she fought prejudice (though some argue she could have done more) and treated it with the contempt it deserved. It was her way of confronting racism, of trying to humanise negative 'Britishness', which to a degree she achieved when she won hearts and minds and became 'Mother of the British Army'. Today, the rediscovered portrait of Mary Seacole in profile is proudly displayed at the National Portrait Gallery – which, appropriately, was the former site of the barracks from which the troops bound for the Crimea left in 1854. The painting captures the enigma that is Mary Seacole, and is a powerful evocation of the care-worn but determined face of a matronly, self-possessed humanitarian.

Notes

1 Early Life

1. Mary Seacole, *Wonderful Adventures of Mrs. Seacole in Many Lands* (James Blackwood, London: 1858). The book is also available online: 'Wonderful Adventures of Mrs. Seacole in Many Lands by Mary Seacole', *Project Gutenberg*, http://www.gutenberg.org/ebooks/23031, accessed 4 November 2020.
2. Rex Nettleford, 'Freedom of Thought and Experience: Nineteenth Century West Indian Creole Experience', *Caribbean Quarterly*, Vol. 36, nos 1 and 2 (June 1990).
3. Nettleford, 'Freedom of Thought and Experience'.
4. Nettleford, 'Freedom of Thought and Experience'.
5. Nettleford, 'Freedom of Thought and Experience'.
6. Nettleford, 'Freedom of Thought and Experience'.
7. Nettleford, 'Freedom of Thought and Experience'.
8. Jane Robinson, *Mary Seacole: The Charismatic Black Nurse Who Became a Heroine of the Crimea* (Constable, London: 2005) p 7.

9. Rene Chartrand, *British Forces in the West Indies 1793–1815* (Osprey, London: 1996) p 3.

10. Seacole, *Wonderful Adventures*.

11. Seacole, *Wonderful Adventures*.

12. Ziggi Alexander and Audrey Dewjee, *Mary Seacole: Jamaican National Heroine and 'Doctress' in the Crimean War* (Brent Library Service, London: 1982) p 3.

13. Chartrand, *British Forces in the West Indies*, p 3.

14. Thomas Dancer, *The Medical Assistant; or Jamaican Practice of Physic. Designed Chiefly for the Use of Families and Plantations* (Alexander Aikman, Kingston, Jamaica: 1801) p v.

15. Sir Nicholas Harris Nicolas (ed), *The Dispatches and Letters of Vice-Admiral Lord Viscount Nelson* (Colburn, London: 1844–6), Vol 1, p 34; Christopher Hibbert, *Nelson: A Personal History* (Penguin, London: 1995) p 28; John Bigelow, *Jamaica in 1850* (Putnam, New York: 1851).

16. Seacole, *Wonderful Adventures*.

17. Seacole, *Wonderful Adventures*.

18. Robinson, *Mary Seacole*, p 18.

19. Seacole, *Wonderful Adventures*.

20. See Ron Ramdin, *The Making of the Black Working Class in Britain* (Wildwood House, Aldershot: 1987), and Peter Fryer, *Staying Power: The History of Black People in Britain* (Pluto Press, London: 1984).

21. Ramdin, *The Making of the Black Working Class*, pp 25–8.
22. Seacole, *Wonderful Adventures*.
23. Seacole, *Wonderful Adventures*.
24. Robinson, *Mary Seacole*, pp 30–2.
25. Alexander and Dewjee, *Jamaican National Heroine and 'Doctress' in the Crimean War*, p 3.
26. Seacole, *Wonderful Adventures*.
27. Seacole, *Wonderful Adventures*.
28. Seacole, *Wonderful Adventures*.

2 Business and Nursing

1. Seacole, *Wonderful Adventures*.
2. 'To the Reader' in Seacole, *Wonderful Adventures*.
3. Seacole, *Wonderful Adventures*.
4. Seacole, *Wonderful Adventures*.
5. Seacole, *Wonderful Adventures*.
6. Seacole, *Wonderful Adventures*.
7. Seacole, *Wonderful Adventures*.
8. Seacole, *Wonderful Adventures*.
9. Seacole, *Wonderful Adventures*.
10. Seacole, *Wonderful Adventures*.
11. Seacole, *Wonderful Adventures*.
12. Seacole, *Wonderful Adventures*.
13. Seacole, *Wonderful Adventures*.
14. Seacole, *Wonderful Adventures*.

15. Seacole, *Wonderful Adventures*.

16. Seacole, *Wonderful Adventures*.

17. Seacole, *Wonderful Adventures*.

18. Seacole, *Wonderful Adventures*.

19. Seacole, *Wonderful Adventures*.

20. Seacole, *Wonderful Adventures*.

21. Seacole, *Wonderful Adventures*.

22. Seacole, *Wonderful Adventures*.

23. Seacole, *Wonderful Adventures*.

24. Seacole, *Wonderful Adventures*.

25. Seacole, *Wonderful Adventures*.

26. Seacole, *Wonderful Adventures*.

27. Seacole, *Wonderful Adventures*.

28. Robinson, *Mary Seacole*, p 66.

29. Seacole, *Wonderful Adventures*.

30. Seacole, *Wonderful Adventures*.

31. Seacole, *Wonderful Adventures*.

32. Seacole, *Wonderful Adventures*.

33. Seacole, *Wonderful Adventures*.

34. Seacole, *Wonderful Adventures*.

35. Seacole, *Wonderful Adventures*.

36. Seacole, *Wonderful Adventures*.

37. Seacole, *Wonderful Adventures*.

3 Determined to Serve

1. Seacole, *Wonderful Adventures*.

2. Seacole, *Wonderful Adventures.*

3. Seacole, *Wonderful Adventures.*

4. Seacole, *Wonderful Adventures.*

5. Seacole, *Wonderful Adventures.*

6. Seacole, *Wonderful Adventures.*

7. Seacole, *Wonderful Adventures.*

8. Seacole, *Wonderful Adventures.*

9. Seacole, *Wonderful Adventures.*

10. Seacole, *Wonderful Adventures.*

11. *The Times*, 23 December 1853.

12. Alexander and Dewjee, *Jamaica National Heroine and 'Doctress' in the Crimean War*, p 6.

13. Seacole, *Wonderful Adventures.*

14. Seacole, *Wonderful Adventures.*

15. Seacole, *Wonderful Adventures.*

16. Seacole, *Wonderful Adventures.*

17. Seacole, *Wonderful Adventures.*

18. Seacole, *Wonderful Adventures.*

19. Seacole, *Wonderful Adventures.*

20. Seacole, *Wonderful Adventures.*

21. Seacole, *Wonderful Adventures.*

22. Seacole, *Wonderful Adventures.*

23. Seacole, *Wonderful Adventures.*

24. Seacole, *Wonderful Adventures.*

25. Seacole, *Wonderful Adventures.*

26. Seacole, *Wonderful Adventures.*

27. Seacole, *Wonderful Adventures.*

28. Seacole, *Wonderful Adventures.*

29. Seacole, *Wonderful Adventures*.
30. Seacole, *Wonderful Adventures*.
31. Seacole, *Wonderful Adventures*.
32. Seacole, *Wonderful Adventures*.

4 Onward, At Last

1. Seacole, *Wonderful Adventures*.
2. Seacole, *Wonderful Adventures*.
3. Seacole, *Wonderful Adventures*.
4. Seacole, *Wonderful Adventures*.
5. Seacole, *Wonderful Adventures*.
6. Seacole, *Wonderful Adventures*.
7. Seacole, *Wonderful Adventures*.
8. Seacole, *Wonderful Adventures*.
9. Seacole, *Wonderful Adventures*.
10. Seacole, *Wonderful Adventures*.
11. Seacole, *Wonderful Adventures*.
12. Seacole, *Wonderful Adventures*.
13. Seacole, *Wonderful Adventures*.
14. Seacole, *Wonderful Adventures*.
15. Seacole, *Wonderful Adventures*.
16. Seacole, *Wonderful Adventures*.
17. Seacole, *Wonderful Adventures*.
18. Seacole, *Wonderful Adventures*.
19. Seacole, *Wonderful Adventures*.
20. Seacole, *Wonderful Adventures*.

21. Seacole, *Wonderful Adventures.*
22. Seacole, *Wonderful Adventures.*
23. Seacole, *Wonderful Adventures.*
24. Seacole, *Wonderful Adventures.*
25. Seacole, *Wonderful Adventures.*

5 Prelude to War

1. 'Sick Man of Europe', *Project Gutenberg Self-Publishing Press*, http://self.gutenberg.org/articles/eng/Sick_Man_of_Europe, accessed 27 October 2020.
2. Paul Kerr et al, *The Crimean War* (Boxtree, London: 1997), pp 9–10.
3. John Sweetman, *The Crimean War: 1854–1856* (Bloomsbury Publishing, London: 2014)
4. Kerr et al, *The Crimean War*, pp 13–15.
5. Piers Compton, *Colonel's Lady & Camp Follower: The Story of Women in The Crimean War* (Robert Hale & Company, London: 1970)
6. Compton, *Colonel's Lady & Camp Follower.*
7. Compton, *Colonel's Lady & Camp Follower.*
8. Compton, *Colonel's Lady & Camp Follower.*
9. Compton, *Colonel's Lady & Camp Follower.*
10. Compton, *Colonel's Lady & Camp Follower.*
11. Compton, *Colonel's Lady & Camp Follower.*
12. Compton, *Colonel's Lady & Camp Follower.*

13. Compton, *Colonel's Lady & Camp Follower*; see also Christopher Hibbert, *The Destruction of Lord Raglan* (Longman, London: 1961).

6 The British Hotel

1. Seacole, *Wonderful Adventures*.
2. Seacole, *Wonderful Adventures*.
3. Seacole, *Wonderful Adventures*.
4. Seacole, *Wonderful Adventures*.
5. Seacole, *Wonderful Adventures*.
6. Seacole, *Wonderful Adventures*.
7. Seacole, *Wonderful Adventures*.
8. Seacole, *Wonderful Adventures*.
9. Seacole, *Wonderful Adventures*.
10. Seacole, *Wonderful Adventures*.
11. Seacole, *Wonderful Adventures*.

7 Amidst the Carnage

1. Seacole, *Wonderful Adventures*.
2. Seacole, *Wonderful Adventures*.
3. Seacole, *Wonderful Adventures*.
4. Seacole, *Wonderful Adventures*.
5. Seacole, *Wonderful Adventures*.
6. 'A Stir for Seacole', *Punch*, 6 December 1856.

7. Seacole, *Wonderful Adventures*.

8. Seacole, *Wonderful Adventures*.

9. Seacole, *Wonderful Adventures*.

10. Seacole, *Wonderful Adventures*.

11. Seacole, *Wonderful Adventures*.

12. Seacole, *Wonderful Adventures*.

13. Seacole, *Wonderful Adventures*.

14. Alexis Soyer (eds M Barthorp and E Ray), *A Culinary Campaign* (Southover Press, Lewes: 1995) p 142.

15. Soyer, *A Culinary Campaign*, p 143.

16. Seacole, *Wonderful Adventures*.

17. Seacole, *Wonderful Adventures*.

18. Seacole, *Wonderful Adventures*.

19. Seacole, *Wonderful Adventures*.

20. Seacole, *Wonderful Adventures*.

21. Seacole, *Wonderful Adventures*.

22. Seacole, *Wonderful Adventures*.

23. Seacole, *Wonderful Adventures*.

24. Seacole, *Wonderful Adventures*.

25. Seacole, *Wonderful Adventures*.

26. Seacole, *Wonderful Adventures*.

27. Seacole, *Wonderful Adventures*.

28. Seacole, *Wonderful Adventures*.

29. Seacole, *Wonderful Adventures*.

30. Seacole, *Wonderful Adventures*.

31. Seacole, *Wonderful Adventures*.

32. Seacole, *Wonderful Adventures*.

33. Seacole, *Wonderful Adventures*.
34. Seacole, *Wonderful Adventures*.
35. Seacole, *Wonderful Adventures*.
36. Seacole, *Wonderful Adventures*.
37. Seacole, *Wonderful Adventures*.
38. Seacole, *Wonderful Adventures*.
39. Seacole, *Wonderful Adventures*.
40. Seacole, *Wonderful Adventures*.

8 Aftermath

1. Seacole, *Wonderful Adventures*.
2. Seacole, *Wonderful Adventures*.
3. Seacole, *Wonderful Adventures*.
4. Seacole, *Wonderful Adventures*.
5. Seacole, *Wonderful Adventures*.
6. Seacole, *Wonderful Adventures*.
7. *The Times*, 11 April 1857.
8. Seacole, *Wonderful Adventures*.
9. Seacole, *Wonderful Adventures*.
10. Seacole, *Wonderful Adventures*.
11. Seacole, *Wonderful Adventures*.
12. Seacole, *Wonderful Adventures*.
13. Seacole, *Wonderful Adventures*.
14. Seacole, *Wonderful Adventures*.
15. Seacole, *Wonderful Adventures*.
16. Seacole, *Wonderful Adventures*.

17. Seacole, *Wonderful Adventures*.
18. Seacole, *Wonderful Adventures*.
19. Seacole, *Wonderful Adventures*.
20. Seacole, *Wonderful Adventures*.
21. Seacole, *Wonderful Adventures*.
22. Seacole, *Wonderful Adventures*.
23. Seacole, *Wonderful Adventures*.
24. Seacole, *Wonderful Adventures*.

9 Last Years: Crimean Heroine

1. Robinson, *Mary Seacole*, p 156.
2. *News of the World*, 31 August 1856.
3. *The Times*, 26 August 1856.
4. *Punch*, 25 October 1856.
5. *The Times*, 7 November 1856.
6. *Punch*, 6 December 1856.
7. Robinson, *Mary Seacole*, p 167.
8. W H Russell, quoted in Seacole, *Wonderful Adventures*.
9. Robinson, *Mary Seacole*, p 173.
10. Claydon House Trust Collection, MS/9004/60. Quoted in Robinson, *Mary Seacole*, p 191.
11. Helen Rappaport, 'The Invitation that Never Came: Mary Seacole After the Crimea', *History Today*, Vol. 55 (2005), pp 9–15.

12. Robinson, *Mary Seacole*, p 155; Rappaport, 'The Invitation that Never Came', pp 9–15.
13. Seacole, *Wonderful Adventures*.
14. Seacole, *Wonderful Adventures*.
15. Seacole, *Wonderful Adventures*.
16. Robinson, *Mary Seacole*, pp 197–8.

Further Reading

Autobiography

Seacole, Mary, *Wonderful Adventures of Mary Seacole in Many Lands* (James Blackwood, London: 1858).
_____, (eds Z Alexander and A Dewjee), *Wonderful Adventures of Mary Seacole in Many Lands* (Falling Wall Press, London: 1984).
_____, (ed W Andrews), *Wonderful Adventures of Mary Seacole in Many Lands* (Oxford University Press, New York: 1988).

Published Primary Sources

Bigelow, John, *Jamaica in 1850* (Putnam, New York: 1851).
Blackwood, Lady Alicia, *A Narrative of Personal Experiences [...] Through the Crimean War* (Hatchards, London: 1881).
British Army, *Local Regulations and Orders for the Troops*

Serving in the West India Command and Her Majesty's Colonies on the South American Continent (London: 1843).

Buchanan, George, *Camp Life. As Seen by a Civilian* (Maclehose, Glasgow: 1871).

Buzzard, Thomas, *With the Turkish Army in the Crimea and Asia Minor* (John Murray, London: 1915).

Campbell, Colin Frederick, *Letters from Camp* (Bentley, London: 1894).

Carlyle, Thomas, *Occasional Discourse on the Nigger Question* (Bosworth, London: 1853).

Carmichael, Mrs, *Domestic Manners and Social Conditions of the White, Coloured and Negro Population of the West Indies* (Whittaker and Treacher, London: 1833).

Clifford, Henry, *His Letters and Sketches from the Crimea* (Michael Joseph, London: 1956).

Dancer, Thomas, *The Medical Assistant; or Jamaican Practice of Physic. Designed Chiefly for the Use of Families and Plantations* (Alexander Aikman, Kingston, Jamaica: 1801).

Duberly, Fanny, *Journal Kept During the Russian War* (Longman, London: 1855).

Edgerton, Robert, *Daguerian Excursions in Jamaica* (A Duperly, Kingston, Jamaica: n.d).

Equiano, Olaudah, *The Interesting Narrative of the Life* [...], 2 vols (London: 1789).

Fabens, Joseph W, *A Story of Life on the Isthmus* (Putnam, New York: 1853).

Falconbridge, Ann Maria, *Narrative of Two voyages to the River Sierra Leone during the Years 1791–1792–1793... Also the Present State of the Slave Trade in the West Indies and the Improbability of its Total Abolition* (Higham, London: 1802).

Galt, Edwin, *The Camp and the Cutter; or A Cruise to the Crimea* (Hodgson, London: 1856).

Goodman, Margaret, *Experiences of an English Sister of Mercy* (Smith, Elder, London: 1862).

Griswold, C D, *The Isthmus of Panama and What I Saw There* (Dewitt and Davenport, New York: 1852).

Handbook of Jamaica [...] by Two Members of the Jamaican Civil Service (Kingston: Jamaica Government Printing Establishment, 1881).

Hornby, Lady, *Constantinople during the Crimean War* (Pall Mall Press, London: 1971).

Kelly, Mrs. Tom, *From the Fleet in the Fifties* (Hurst and Blackett, London: 1902).

Montez, Lola, *Autobiography and Lectures* (James Blackwood, London: 1858).

Nelson, Admiral Lord Horatio, *The Letters of Lord Nelson and Lady Hamilton* (Thomas Lovewell, London: 1814).

Nicolas, Sir Nicholas Harris (ed), *The Dispatches and Letters of Vice-Admiral Lord Viscount Nelson* (Colburn, London: 1844–6).

Nugent, Lady Maria (ed P Wright), *Lady Nugent's Journal of Her Residence in Jamaica from 1801–1805* (Institute of Jamaica, Kingston, Jamaica: 1966).

Prince, Mary, *The History of Mary Prince: A West Indian Slave related by Herself* (Westleigh and Davis, London; Waugh and Innis, Edinburgh: 1831).

Reid, Douglas Arthur, *Memories of the Crimean War* (St. Catherine's Press, London: 1911).

Robins, Major Colin, *Captain Dunscombe's Diary: The Real Crimean War* (Withycut House, Bowdon: 2003).

Russell, Sir William Howard (ed N Bentley), *Russell's Despatches from the Crimea 1854–1856* (Deutsch, London: 1996).

Simpson, William, *The Seat of the War in the East from Eighty-one Drawings made During the War in the Crimea* (Day and Son, London: 1902).

_____, (ed G Eyre-Todd) *The Autobiography of William Simpson RI* (T. Fisher Unwin, London: 1903).

Soyer, Alexis, (eds M Barthorp and E Ray), *A Culinary Campaign* (Southover Press, Lewes: 1995).

Terrot, Sarah Anne (ed R G Richardson), *Nurse Sarah Anne. With Florence Nightingale at Scutari* (John Murray, London: 1977).

Vicars, Captain Hedley (ed C Marsh), *Memorials* [...] (James Nisbet, London: 1856).

Vieth, Frederick, *Recollections of the Crimean Campaign* (John Lovell, Montreal: 1907).

Secondary Sources

Alexander, Ziggi, and Audrey Dewjee, *Mary Seacole. Jamaican National Heroine and 'Doctress' in the Crimean War* (Brent Library Service, London: 1982).

Ayensu, E, *Medicinal Plants of the West Indies* (Reference Publications, Algonac: 1981).

Backhouse, Francis (ed), *Women of the Klondike* (White Cap, Vancouver: 1995).

Baker, Christopher, *Jamaica* (Lonely Planet, London: 2000).

Bolt, Christine, *Victorian Attitudes to Race* (Routledge and Keegan Paul, London: 1971).

Bonham Carter, Violet (ed), *Surgeon in the Crimea* (Michael Joseph, London: 1956).

Braithwaite, Edward, *The Development of Creole Society in Jamaica 1770–1820* (Clarendon Press, Oxford: 1971).

Briggs, Asa, *Victorian People 1851–1867* (Chicago University Press, Chicago: 1970).

Brooke, Elisabeth, *Women Healers through History* (Women's Press, London: 1993).

Carnegie, M E, 'Black Nurses at the Front', *American Journal of Nursing*, Vol. 84 (1984).

Chartrand, Rene, *British Forces in the West Indies 1793– 1815* (Osprey, London: 1996).

Coleman, Terry, *Nelson* (Bloomsbury, London: 2001).

Compton, Piers, *Colonel's Lady and Camp Follower. The*

Story of Women in the Crimean War (Robert Hale & Company, London: 1970).

Cook, E, *The Life of Florence Nightingale* (Macmillan, London: 1914).

Cooper, Helen, 'England: The Imagined Community of Aurora Leigh and Mrs. Seacole', *Studies in Browning and His Circle*, Vol. 20 (1993).

Crawford, P, 'The Other Lady With the Lamp', *Nursing Times*, Vol. 88, no 11 (1992).

Delany, A, *A History of the Catholic Church in Jamaica* (Jesuit Press, New York: 1930).

Edwards, Paul, and David Dabydeen (eds), *Black Writers in Britain 1760–1890* (Edinburgh: Edinburgh University Press, 1991).

Ffrench-Blake, R, *The Crimean War* (Cooper, London: 1971).

File, Nigel, and Chris Power, *Black Settlers in Britain 1555–1958* (Heinemann, London: 1981).

Fish, Cheryl, *Black and White Women's Travel Narratives* (University Press of Florida, Gainesville: 2004).

Fletcher, Ian and Natalia Ischenko, *The Crimean War: A Clash of Empires* (Spellmount, Staplehurst: 2004).

Fraser, Flora, *Beloved Emma. The Life of Emma, Lady Hamilton* (Wiedenfeld and Nicholson, London: 1994).

Frederick, Rhona, 'Creole Performance in Wonderful Adventures of Mrs. Seacole in Many Lands', *Gender and History*, Vol. 15, no 3 (2004).

Fryer, Peter, *Staying Power. The History of Black People in Britain* (Pluto Press, London: 1984).

Gernsheim, Helmut and Alison, *Roger Fenton: Photographer of the Crimean War* (Secker and Warburg, London: 1954).

Gerzina, Gretchen, *Black England. Life Before Emancipation* (John Murray, London: 1995).

Gikaandi, Simon, *Maps of Englishness. Writing Identity in the Culture of Colonialism* (Columbia University Press, New York: 1996).

Golby, J M, *Culture and Society in Britain 1850–1890* (Oxford University Press, Oxford: 1986).

Goldie, Sue, *Calendar of the Letters of Florence Nightingale* (Oxford Microforms, Oxford: 1983).

_____(ed), *'I Have Done My Duty': Florence Nightingale in the Crimean War 1854–1856* (Manchester University Press, Manchester: 1987).

Gustafson, M, 'Mary Seacole, the Florence Nightingale of Jamaica,' *Christian Nurse International*, Vol. 12, no 4 (1996).

Hawthorn, Evelyn, 'Self-Writing, Literary Traditions and Post-Emancipation Identity: The Case of Mary Seacole,' *Biography*, Vol. 23, no 2 (2000).

Henriques, Fernando, *Children of Caliban: Miscegenation* (Secker and Warburg, London: 1964).

Hibbert, Christopher, *The Destruction of Lord Raglan* (Longman, London: 1961).

_____, Nelson. A Personal History (Penguin, London: 1995).

Hume, Hamilton, The Life of Edward John Eyre, Late Governor of Jamaica (Bentley, London: 1867).

Hurwitz, Samuel and Edith, Jamaica. A Historical Portrait (Pall Mall Press, London: 1971).

Innes, C L, A History of Black and Asian Writing in Britain, 1700–2000 (Cambridge University Press, Cambridge: 1992).

Iveson-Iveson, J, 'The Forgotten Heroine', Nursing Mirror, Vol. 157 (1983).

Josephs, Aleric, 'Mary Seacole: Jamaican Nurse and "Doctress"', Jamaican Historical Review, Vol. 17 (1991).

Judd, Catherine, Bedside Seductions. Nursing and the Victorian Imagination 1830–1880 (Macmillan, London: 1998).

Kerr, Paul et al, The Crimean War (Boxtree, London: 1997).

Khan, H, 'Remembering Mary Seacole', West Indian Digest (June 1981).

King, A, 'Mary Seacole,' Essence, Vol. 4, nos 11 and 12 (1974).

Kinglake, A W, The Invasion of the Crimea (Blackwood, Edinburgh: 1863–87).

Laguerre, Michel, Afro-Caribbean Folk Medicine (Bergin and Garvey, South Hadley: 1987).

Long, Edward, *The History of Jamaica* (Cass, London: 1970).

Lorimer, Douglas, *Colour, Class and the Victorians. English Attitudes to the Negro in the Mid-Nineteenth Century* (Leicester University Press, Leicester: 1978).

Malam, John, *Tell Me More About Pioneers: Mary Seacole* (Evans, London: 1999).

McKenna, Bernard, 'Fancies of Exclusive Possession: Validation and Dissociation in Mary Seacole's England and Caribbean', *Philological Quarterly*, Vol. 76, no 2 (1997).

Messmer, P R, and Y Parchment, 'Mary Grant Seacole: The first Nurse Practitioner', *Clinical Excellence for Nurse Practitioners*, Vol. 2, no 1 (1998).

Mills, Therese, *Great West Indians* (Longman Carribean, Kingston: 1973).

Moorcroft, Christine, and Magnus Magnusson: *Famous People: Mary Seacole 1805–1881* (Channel 4, London: 1998).

Moore, Henry Charles, *Noble Deeds of the World's Heroines* (Religious Tract Society, London: 1903).

Morris, Helen, *Portrait of a Chef* (Oxford University Press, Oxford: 1980).

Nettleford, Rex, 'Freedom of Thought and Experience: Nineteenth Century West Indian Creole Experience', *Caribbean Quarterly*, Vol. 36, nos 1 and 2 (June 1990).

Paquet, Sandra Pouchon, 'Mary Seacole: The Enigma of Arrival', *African American Review*, Vol. 26, no 4 (1992).

Pollitt, N, 'Forgotten Heroine', *Times Higher Educational Supplement*, no 3965 (1992).

Pritchard, R E (ed), *Dickens's England. Life in Victorian Times* (Sutton, Stroud: 2002).

Ramdin, Ron, *The Making of the Black Working Class in Britain* (Wildwood House, Aldershot: 1987).

_____, *Reimaging Britain: 500 Years of Black and Asian History* (Pluto Press, London: 1999).

Rappaport, Helen, 'The Invitation that Never Came: Mary Seacole After the Crimea', *History Today*, Vol. 55 (February 2005), pp 9–15.

Robinson, Amy, 'Authority and the Public Display of Identity: Wonderful Adventures of Mrs. Seacole in Many Lands', *Feminist Studies*, Vol. 20, no 3 (1994).

Robinson, Jane, *Wayward Women: A Guide to Women Travellers* (Oxford University Press, Oxford: 1990).

_____, *Mary Seacole: The Charismatic Black Nurse Who Became a Heroine of the Crimea* (Constable, London: 2005).

Scobie, James, *Black Britannia: A History of Blacks in Britain* (Johnson Publishing, Chicago: 1972).

Seymour, Bruce, *Lola Montez. A Life* (Yale University Press, New Haven: 1996).

Shepherd, John, *The Crimean Doctors. A History of the British Medical Services in the Crimean War* (Liverpool University Press, Liverpool: 1991).

Sheridan, Richard, *Doctors and Slaves. A Medical and Demographic History of Slavery in the British West*

Indies 1680–1834 (Cambridge University Press, Cambridge: 1985).

Shyllon, F O, *Black People in Britain, 1555–1833* (Institute of Race Relations/Oxford University Press, London: 1977).

Small, Hugh, *Florence Nightingale: Avenging Angel* (Constable, London: 1998).

Smith, J P, 'Mary Jane Seacole', *Journal of Advanced Nursing*, Vol. 9, no 5 (1984).

Summers, Anne, *Angels and Citizens. British Women as Military Nurses 1854–1914* (Routledge and Keegan Paul, London: 1988).

Sweetman, John, *The Crimean War* (Osprey, Oxford: 2001).

Tisdall, E E P, *Mrs. Duberly's Campaigns* (Jarrolds, London: 1963).

Vernon, C, 'The Story of Mary Seacole', *Jamaican Nurse*, Vol. 25 (1986).

Vulliamy, C, *Crimea. The Campaign of 1854–56* (Cape, London: 1939).

Walvin, James, *Black and White: The Negro and English Society, 1555–1945* (Allen Lane, London: 1973).

Woodham Smith, Cecil, *Florence Nightingale 1820–1910* (Constable, London: 1950).

Index